SAMMY

HAGAR

BIOGRAPHY

The Inside Story of the Red Years

CONTENTS

CHAPTER 1

MOBILE HOME BLUES

Ed Mattson taught me to play the guitar and drive. Ed was three years my senior and had attended the same school as my brother. Ed had been this chubby boy with a large nose in high school. Ed then had a nose operation in Hollywood, went on a diet, and lost a lot of weight. His mother purchased him a new 1962 Chevrolet Super Sport Impala. He was suddenly the coolest guy in town, yet no one knew who he was. My brother had no idea who he was. He had a fantastic pompadour. He was a guitarist who grew up listening to Bob Dylan. Ed introduced me to the Beatles and the Rolling Stones. Elvis had been my first true hero since my older sisters adored him so much. My sisters used to throw parties when I was a kid. They'd dress me up, ducktail me, and every single one of those gals would dance with me. I dug it up to the bone. I was a little hard-on, a nine-year-old kid with these females who were five or six years older, getting sexy, getting little titties. It was all due to Elvis.

Despite my admiration for Elvis, I never pursued a career in music. But the Beatles had an effect on me. I was in high school and already had a girlfriend, but I couldn't get enough of "I Want to Hold Your Hand." I was gone when I heard the Stones. In June 1964, local Top 40 DJ George Babcock invited the Rolling Stones to San Bernardino for the band's debut concert in America, and I fucking went. Ed Mattson and I drove over to the Swing Auditorium in his car with the intention of sneaking in. We were standing outside the back door when this clumsy, messed-up orange school bus arrived, and George Babcock got off with the Stones. They came in through the rear entrance, and we followed straight behind them.

That's when it all started for me. I knew I wanted to be a musician that night. Ed Mattson already knew how to play the guitar. I began singing with him, and we would listen to Beatles and Stones tunes.

We only knew maybe three or four songs. Ed stated that we needed two guitars so that he could play lead. My mom had a job and was doing well by that point, so I tried to persuade her into purchasing me a guitar on her Sears account. She promised to purchase me a guitar if I learned to play "Never on Sunday," the popular foreign film title track played on a bouzouki on Ed's guitar. I figured it out in a day or two. She purchased it on time. A Silvertone guitar and amplifier in a case cost $39.95.

I barely got through high school after discovering rock-and-roll and pussy. I was done, especially after I acquired my first guitar. I was failing every class. "Why don't you apply yourself?" my teachers would remark. That was back in high school. I was just interested in music and females.

And when I eventually got high, it was all over. My friend and I smoked a joint and drove down a dirt road in the Jurupa Hills, almost to Riverside. I couldn't help but laugh. I was unable to drive. I couldn't do anything. It appealed to me. After I decided I wanted to smoke dope, you had to find the lowlifes of all lowlifes in order to get that dope. These were the Fontana dope dealers—not hippies, but bad-guy heroin dealers—to whom you went if you wanted to purchase some cannabis. It wasn't even decent marijuana. So I became a stoner, smoking marijuana every day, ingesting acid, and even shooting speed. I tried heroin and didn't like it.

I wanted to be a musician, but I worked in the automotive department at ABC Stores. I had this girlfriend, Christie Carson, who looked like Twiggy, and I wore my hair in a Bob Dylan Afro. I began living with her in San Bernardino at her grandmother's house. My mom cosigned for and I was making payments on a brand-new black 1967 Volkswagen—$1,900 out the door less $300 trade-in. I persuaded the ABC Store manager to develop a music department at the Riverside location, which I ran. I purchased all of the records. I began collecting record players. I began stocking guitars. I created the entire music department. But I was a drug user. I was always smoking dope. I was stoned the entire time. I would get up in the morning and smoke roaches before going to work.

The concert was held within a fenced-in stadium surrounded by a park. Thousands of people had gathered outside. I spent the majority of my time outside the arena, in the park. When Bucky introduced me to Fresh Cream, I knew exactly what I wanted to accomplish. I hadn't worked in a while, and I'd been spending my days getting high. I'd been listening to East-West by the Paul Butterfield Blues Band and, of course, Sergeant Pepper's, but not really trying to play anything, just tripping. But then Cream released their debut album, and I realised I needed to get back into music. I wasn't just hallucinating anymore. I went and stole a guitar, or rather, a friend of mine did. He was aware of the guitar and its location. We waited for the people to leave their house before climbing through their back window. My pal did it because he thought I'd become a rock star.

THE NEXT MONTH, I went to see a band I'd heard about. They already had a lead vocalist who played guitar and was quite talented, and I had only gone to see them. I entered in a pinstriped double-breasted jacket with a roach clip on my lapel, a white T-shirt, trousers, boots, John Lennon sunglasses, and my frizzy Afro haircut. Jesse Llamas, the band's guitarist, took one glance at me and asked, "Can you sing?" I was the new singer for the Mobile Home Blues Band in an instant.

CHAPTER 2

GOING TO SAN FRANCISCO

Bucky's girlfriend came in with his sister, Betsy, one night with a couple of bogus IDs. On the break, I brought them sloe gin fizzes because it seemed like a girly drink. She may have had two. Betsy became dizzy, so I carried her outdoors and cradled her in my arms. She had never had a cocktail in her life. She'd never done drugs before. I fell in love with her while standing there holding her. I was still staying at Christie's grandmother's house, but I began hanging out with Betsy and shortly ended my relationship with Christie. It wasn't long before Betsy and I decided to marry on a camping trip to Big Sur. On November 3, 1968, I was twenty-one years old and we married.

This was Betsy and my honeymoon when we married. We discovered hotel rooms on Broadway above Basin Street West. Betsy and I had our own room, while the other guys shared one. The restroom was located down the hall. I wasn't a junkie, but I decided I'd had enough of drugs and tried to clean myself. I didn't want to smoke marijuana anymore because Betsy didn't like it. I'd get stoned and depressed, so I tried to avoid it entirely.

This was difficult because there was always a lot of cannabis around. It came in pounds. Larry Taylor, the drummer, had never taken acid before we arrived in San Francisco, but not long after we arrived, he took LSD and went walking around the streets. "You guys want to get high?" he asks two cops walking the beat on Broadway. "Sure," they say, "we'd like to get stoned." He brings the two cops back to our house at four o'clock in the morning—thank goodness Betsy and I had our separate room. Larry and Dave were fucked up and arrested. So that band was obviously over.

I was seeking for any means to make money. I used to be in a band called Salt and Pepper with Herb Gross. When Herb first approached me about joining his band, I told him I needed money, so he got me a job at H. H. Sullivan Printing Company. I got off the dump truck at eight a.m., ate breakfast, and then proceeded to work at H. H. Sullivan until five o'clock in the afternoon. I'd work overtime if there was any available. At the same time, I practised every night with Salt and Pepper. We never performed live, but we practised the entire time I was there. During this time, I was drafted, and because Betsy was pregnant, I turned in her medical report. They did not draft any men with children. That was the Woodstock summer. I wanted to go because it was just across the state, but Betsy was too pregnant.

That summer, I worked nonstop. I saved every money and did not spend a single dime. We ate at the house for gratis. I did not purchase a record. I did not purchase a guitar string. I did not purchase a candy bar. I constantly told Betsy's folks that I wanted to return to California and that I wasn't going to take any chances. Betsy's father custom-built this van for us to travel back to California. He installed a brand-new engine and transmission, as well as some great, fresh tires, in this old, beat-up van. He, Bucky, and I collaborated on it. I worked two jobs, was in a band, and spent my weekends working on my automobile. I was ready to go the first time I started that car. Bucky placed our shit in the back and then jumped in with Betsy and me at the last second. He didn't even kiss his parents goodbye. His father intended to murder him. It was four o'clock in the afternoon on the first day of snow in Rochester that year. I had my cash. We fucked split the second that engine fired up.

Aaron was born on February 24th, 1970. Betsy went nuts almost immediately after giving birth. She had a nervous breakdown and panic attacks that left her unable to breathe. She was in critical condition and was admitted to Ward B of San Bernardino County Hospital. She needs the services of a therapist.

My sister Bobbi took after little Aaron while Betsy was in pain, and I managed to ignore what was going on around me. My wife is having a nervous breakdown. I was twenty-one, had just had a baby, and still had a one-track mind. Nothing else meant as much to me as music, not even my wife or my new son. Every day, I was playing music with Big Bang and looking for nighttime gigs. We did a few gigs here and there. We played six sets a night at the Hat Factory in Riverside, starting at 10 p.m. and finishing at 6 a.m. We won a Battle of the Bands by performing "Manic Depression." We were presented with a trophy and a teardrop Vox electric guitar, which we exchanged for public-address equipment. We eventually settled on Jeff Nicholson, a young college student with a boyish appearance.

Finally, Betsy's psychiatrist asked me to see her or we'd be taken off welfare. He needed to find out what was going on. I told him I wanted to be a big rock star. He addressed me as Peter Pan. "You need to wake up, son, and go out there and get a job," he told him. "You've got a wife and a child." He went after me hard. That simply infuriated me. I was ready to take him outside. I was completely confident in myself. I was adamant about succeeding. But, with my long hair, bad attitude, no job, on welfare, a baby, and my wife in the hospital, I could have come across as a complete jerk. When Betsy was born, my sister Bobbi nursed her back to health and was a tremendous help to her. I didn't make any modifications.

I'd first seen the flashy guitarist a week or so earlier, when I went to see the Edgar Winter Band at Winterland in San Francisco with the rest of the Justice Brothers, who were there to see Tower of Power, which was also on the bill. I was all jewelled up because it was a rare night off from the Wharf Rat. I was looking forward to seeing Edgar

Winter because he was a glitter rocker. That was all the information I required. Even though Ronnie Montrose had previously been recording with Van Morrison, I had seen him on TV and liked his motions. He did this little trick where he knelt down with his Les Paul and spun in a circle, leaning on one foot. He circled and circled. He did not become entangled in his cord. It was a wise decision. I was blown away.

The next day, I started hammering the guys in the band, telling them that's the type of guitarist we need. We weren't getting along all that well already, but everyone wanted to keep the solid employment. I'd discussed it with John Blakeley, one of the few men from Riverside I knew who was in a band called Stoneground, but I didn't even know Winter's guitarist's name.

"That's Ronnie Montrose," Blakeley identified. "He is from Sausalito." That was his final performance with Edgar Winter. He's on the lookout for a singer."

So I ended up knocking on Montrose's door while dressed in a silver suit and boots. I brought four songs that I had written that the Justice Brothers refused to perform. He connected me into his little amp, and I sang "Bad Motor Scooter," "Make It Last," "I Don't Want It," and "One Thing on My Mind." He only had the riff to "Rock the Nation"—that was all he had. I showed him the lyrics to "Space Station Number 5" and he immediately began playing that riff. That day, we wrote the song together.

I assumed he was wealthy. From where I was standing, he appeared to be a member of the world's biggest band. They'd sold out stadiums and had a number one album. What was I thinking? I had no idea the place was for rent. I noticed his automobile, a 1963 Ford four-door, outside. I noticed he was driving a beat-up car, but it didn't bother me. All I knew was that he'd just deposited a $8,000 royalty check—a fortune in my opinion.

10

The Justice Brothers were furious when Ronnie came to see me at the Wharf Rat, but they kissed his ass. He strolled in wearing a crushed-velvet jacket and large rings on his fingers. We went outside after the set and he said, "Let's start a band." That night, I left the Justice Brothers. Nicholson was wearing my exact clothes a week later. He had Betsy sew the garments for him. He's got the glitter, the makeup, the entire shebang. He's impersonating me.

Ronnie inquired as to whether I knew any drummers. I sang on a demo tape by this band, Thunderstick, a while back. They sounded a lot like Free, a lot like Paul Rodgers, and nothing like Northern California. They sounded like English glitter-rock but didn't see it. They were all dressed casually in jeans and T-shirts. I had the expression. They were desperate for me. They didn't have a record deal, but they did have a record company representative who was intrigued but didn't like their singer. I made some demos with them and was considering joining them, but no one in the Justice Brothers, not even me, wanted to lose the Wharf Rat gig. Then I came across Edgar Winter at Winterland. Thunderstick's drummer was Denny Carmassi. Denny earned the job despite the fact that we tried out the legendary British rock drummer Aynsley Dunbar. Ronnie didn't want any rivalry. Ronnie desired power, so he sought out people like me, who knew nothing. We went to Studio Instrument Rentals and auditioned a few bassists, including Andy Fraser of Free, who turned out to be a total junkie and never showed up. Before joining Journey, we tried Ross Valory and Pete Sears of Jefferson Starship. Bill Church was a friend of Ronnie's from the Van Morrison band and, before that, a member of a band named Sawbuck that appeared on various Fillmore shows. Chuck Ruff, Edgar Winter's drummer, was also a Sawbuck member. Church sat there the entire time, watching us experiment with all these guys. I kept telling Ronnie how much I like Church.

"Yeah, but the guy's kind of an asshole," he said.

Through Van Morrison, Ronnie met Ted Templeman of Warner Bros. Records. Ted noticed us and walked over to us. We rehearsed three or four times at Studio Instrument Rental and had the entire first record written. We aspired to be the next Deep Purple or Led Zeppelin.

"Rock Candy" was the final song we composed. We had nine songs, one titled "Drugs" and another titled "We're Flying," that weren't very good and were discarded. We needed one more good tune, Templeman said. Denny had just begun playing that drum beat when Ted entered the room. Ronnie came up with the riff, and all I could think was, "You're rock candy, baby." The song simply sort of came together. That was the sole song written by the band. The rest of the tracks were written by Ronnie or me.

Ted agreed to sign us. We immediately entered the studio with him and engineer Donn Landee. Everything happened so quickly. We relocated to the Sheraton Burbank, close to the Warner Bros. lot, where all of the acts remained. We didn't have any money. We were given a $50,000 advance, but we had to spend $25,000 on equipment. We each took $5,000. We kept $5,000 in the bank. We didn't have a boss. Ronnie was in complete command.

I received my $5,000. I rented a house in Mill Valley for $80 per month at 37 Montford Street, and I got an automobile. Of course, not just any automobile, but a Citroën Deux Chevaux, the world's most uncool car—a French car that looks like a sardine can. It struck me as formal. I sold my Volkswagen to a guy for $50. The van was so poor that when I sold it, it couldn't even get out of the driveway. It was too high. Because it couldn't make it, the person had to back up in the dirt and get a running start. It was that helpless. The Citroen was nearly three grand. I rented the house and had about $1,200 in savings. I was wealthy. We made some session money while working on the CD. I finally had a phone. I received my first credit card. I knew the album was going to be released, and I had written the songs for it. Ronnie did a great thing for me by having our lawyer put up my own publishing business, Big Bang Music, so that I could control my publication rights.

CHAPTER 3

MONTROSE

The first Montrose album never charted. It spent one week on Bubbling Under, but it never made it to the Billboard album charts. We sold eighty thousand records by the end of the tour. In New York, I went into Dee Anthony's office and said, "Hey, Dee, Ted Templeman told me we've sold eighty thousand records." "Frank, these guys sold eighty thousand records," he said as he picked up the phone and dialled the booking agency. Let's start with $75 and work our way up to $1,000."

It only sold slowly, but it did sell. When we first came out, we didn't have a big Top 40 hit, but FM was picking up on "Space Station" and "Rock Candy." Although it has never charted, the first Montrose album has sold more than 4 million copies over the years. "Rock Candy" has become a staple for bands such as Def Leppard and the Cult. We had a lot of money problems by the time we finished the tour. All of that per diem things got erratic about a month into the trip, and when we finished the first tour, we were owed ten weeks' back pay. Dee Anthony had helped us a little, but not a lot. We ran out of money while driving. We got stuck in a Holiday Inn in Little Rock, Arkansas, and couldn't get out because Ronnie's credit card was full. They summoned the cops and ordered us to remain in the filthy hotel. We dialled Dee Anthony's number, and he eventually gave them a credit card over the phone. We were making $500 per night and touring cost around $600 each night. We were on the verge of death. My house phone was disconnected because I had not been paid.

When we got off the road for the second record, Denny and I went into this little basement studio I had and wrote a bunch of tunes. I wrote "Call My Name," "Someone Out There," and a few more songs for my debut solo album, Nine on a Ten Scale. I wrote them for Montrose, but Ronnie refused to listen to them. He didn't want me to take over the band. I didn't want to be in charge of his band, but I was determined to succeed. I thought I had a brilliant plan for that band. It may not have been the best idea. I wouldn't say Ronnie was completely wrong. But he became so self-conscious about it that he ended a wonderful literary partnership. He had the ability to nurture me. That was one of my early tunes.

My marriage was on the rocks while all of this was going on with Montrose. Betsy, my wife, was in tears. Despite her collapse after Aaron's birth, I had no idea how serious her psychiatric issues were. She was quite needy, and I liked how it made me feel. When the band started doing a little better, I told her she could come out on the road with me. Ronnie had a firm rule against wives on tour, but I told him I didn't have a choice. The first time we went to England, she borrowed money from her parents and flew to England on her own.

In Europe, Ronnie wouldn't talk to me. Montrose headlined some shows. Other nights, we would open for the other bands, like the Doobie Brothers. We opened for Little Feat in Amsterdam and got booed off the stage by the third song. People started whistling in the middle of our songs. That really destroyed Ronnie. He decided it was over. I could see it in his head. He wanted to break up the band. I knew it. I heard him talking to Denny.

The next day, on the plane on the way home, I talked to Denny about starting another band. A week later, Ronnie called him and the other guys and told them he was going to keep Montrose together and get a new singer. It was totally premeditated. He had it all figured out. Our record deal was up, and he had already told Ted Templeman that he wanted to renew the record contract and that he was getting a new singer. They were going to re-sign for a lot more money.

I got home from that tour with nothing in my pocket, no money in the bank. My wife was freaking out and I had nothing going on, nothing coming up. I didn't think I could make my next month's rent. But almost immediately, a publishing royalty check from the first Montrose album, for $5,100, showed up in the mail. I had no record deal. I had no way to make a living, except for playing music. I knew I was going to be okay, but I didn't have it set in stone. So I went out and I bought a $5,000 Porsche.

CHAPTER 4

THE RED ROCKER

I walked into my sister's house after being fired and immediately dialled the phone. Betsy had returned to Europe, and Bobbi had been caring for Aaron. I drove directly from the airport to her house. I took up the phone and contacted Dee Anthony to inform him that Ronnie had dismissed me. "Hold on," he advised. "Don't drop any bombs on me." I need to look into this. You owe me a lot of cash." Dee was never heard from again. Jerry Berg, Dee Anthony's tour manager, was always fond of me. He quit his job to manage me when I told him I needed a manager. He was a first-rate gentleman, usually well-dressed. He handled the money, and I assumed he knew what he was doing. He appeared to be a good businessman, but he had no idea what he was doing managing a band. Dee Anthony had been taking care of everything while keeping Jerry in the dark.

I wrote and wrote and wrote some more. Bill Church jumped on board right on since he disliked Ronnie for firing him from Montrose. When Denny couldn't come over any longer, I began bringing his younger brother, Billy Carmassi. Glenn Campbell from the band Juicy Lucy was my slide player. He'd been playing around Riverside before arriving in England, and he'd just finished the Mad Dogs and Englishmen Tour with Joe Cocker and Leon Russell. In those days, all I knew how to accomplish was what I'd done with Montrose. That was the start of my independent years. I just knew how to be Montrose in the absence of Ronnie. I was singing and playing the guitar. I was incredibly motivated to make my own songs and tour till I made it. I didn't consider it a hit.

Ted Templeman was the first person I called. The only person I knew in the record business was the Warner Bros. staff producer who worked on the two Montrose albums. He refused to sign me as a solo artist, but Ted did give me a few thousand bucks to demo some songs. I went to Wally Heider's studio and recorded "Silver Lights," a number of other songs I'd written for Montrose, and a handful of new songs. Jerry and I went down to San Francisco FM rock radio station KSAN, and thank God for radio stations like that back then. They performed my five-song demo and broadcast it live. I didn't even have the rights to the tunes, but it didn't matter. John Carter was somewhere out there and heard it.

When I stepped in one night, the person at the front desk was using nitrous oxide. Carter's engineer was also using nitrous oxide while mixing the album. He chose a song called "All American" and had everyone overdub while I was gone. He multiplied everything. He doubled the bass, as well as the drums. He combined two twenty-four-tracks. The next day, he played it for me. It wobbled and was out of sync. As if the nitrous wasn't bad enough, these guys had just returned from a two-day coke/weed run. I threw it away. I was about to leave the studio one day when I heard a buzz at the door. I buzzed the person at the door because the receptionist on nitrous was nowhere to be found. It had to be Van Morrison.

"Fucking drug addicts," he grumbled as he strolled by the front desk. I ran after him.

"Van, I'm Sammy Hagar," I introduced myself. "I'm doing a record with John Carter"—he knew Carter—"do you have any songs?"

"Like what?" he inquired.

"Like in 'Into the Mystic,'" I explained. It was one of my favourite Van songs.

"Follow me," he instructed.

He chose an acoustic guitar and we entered a little room. He put on "Flamingos Fly." Giving it up is not the same as going through the motions. Eyes closed, singing my heart out. I'm getting goosebumps. This guy was my hero at the time, my favourite songwriter—him and John Lennon were the ones I wanted to write like. He promised to return the following day and record the song for me. I'd been jacked out of my head. Carter freaked out when I informed him. Van Morrison returned the following day in a different mood. He got down at a microphone without a click track, played acoustic guitar, and performed the song for a demo. He couldn't have cared less this time. He smashed it and split. Carter, on the other hand, has a brilliant idea. We had Steely Dan's Jimmy Hodder overdub drums, Bill Church overdub bass (he'd previously performed with Van), and me sing on this track, and we made it sound like a duet between myself and Van Morrison. We were about to release that record until Van caught wind of it. His attorneys quickly removed him from the record. We had to return at the last minute and start over on that song. My debut album, Nine on a Scale of Ten, was completed and released in May 1976. I went on tour almost soon with Joe Cocker, Ted Nugent, and a slew of other artists. I opened the door for everyone. They stopped selling that record after 27,000 copies. It was no longer in print. It wasn't because it was dying. It didn't fare well, but there was some backstage politics with Dee Anthony, who still believed I owed him money from Montrose and wielded enormous power in the industry, which killed it at the label. As a result, I parted ties with Jerry Berg and went on with Ed Leffler, who would manage my career for the remainder of his life.

While we were working on the second album, I wrote the song "Red." Carter revised some of the lyrics. I would listen to him because he was good with lyrics. He was more poetic than I was. Carter used the phrase "crimson sin intensity" in one of his sentences. That was clever and kind of deep, in my opinion. I began wearing red and painting my instruments red. I started turning red, red, red. I recently discovered that I adore the colour red.

I was offered the Kiss tour at the last minute, just before the January 1977 release of the Red record (official title: Sammy Hagar). I was added on the bill at Madison Square Garden in New York that February so late that I wasn't even advertised on the performance. Before I walked out, people began booing. Except for Montrose, I'd never played in New York. They had no idea who I was. When I looked around, the entire restaurant was decked out in Kiss garb. They've all put on makeup. They were booing and yelling at me. I did a $1-admission show called the Rising Star in Seattle shortly after the Red album was released, as part of a radio station promotion conducted by some Northwest disc jockeys. It was effective for me. I sold out, and the Northwest was one of my first major markets.

The newspaper reviewer who covered the Rising Star event dubbed me "The Red Rocker, Sammy Hagar." Some kid approached me with a newspaper and asked me to sign it. "Will you sign it 'The Red Rocker'?" he asked. I was content only to sign an autograph. A few days later, I was going down the street in Texas when I heard someone say, "Hey, it's The Red Rocker." And then it hit me: "Hey, that's me."

On that first little headline tour, I did the craziest thing. I made a live album, All Night Long, and that became my next release in 1978. Oddly enough, the live album sold about 250,000 records. I was starting to break. You could see it. My record was selling with no singles, no radio airplay, no nothing. Just twenty-one months of non stop touring. I'd made an album every year for the previous five years at Capitol, while continually touring. I'd get off the road and go into the studio. When I wasn't touring, I was working on an album. The label paid for tour support, but because my records weren't selling well and I was always on the road, I couldn't cover the costs. I'd done well in England and other European countries, but Capitol never gave me a penny. In fact, they informed me that I owed them $175,000. I had a terrible record deal. I was making around twenty cents on every record. I was spending more money than I was earning on tour. I made the decision to sue Capitol.

John Kalodner, Geffen Records' big-cheese A&R man, wanted to sign me to the label David Geffen had just launched. He had only signed John Lennon and Donna Summer at the time. They made me a million-dollar offer. Capitol was paying me $50,000 for each album and I owed them money, but the money Geffen gave me paid for the litigation. We arrived at Marin Civic Center court one day, and the judge said to Capitol, "I think you folks have made enough money off this young fella." He let me out of the contract. I was a free man when I left. Geffen pushed me to the top of the charts. I finally had hit records that matched my road box office. Capitol was never able to accomplish this. Capital did not promote me. They couldn't care less. It was especially sweet when I signed with Geffen and smacked Capitol in the face with my first gold and platinum album. That marked the start of a sixteen-year run of million-seller albums. Kalodner was the best A&R person ever. He persuaded Survivor's Jimmy Peterik to co-write a song with me, "Heavy Metal," and sold it to the film before my CD was even released. I was in a band. I had a team.

Success really inspired me. I used the remainder of Geffen's large cash advance to begin purchasing property in Fontana. We constructed nine residential structures. I bought the old houses we used to rent when I was a kid. That was my first foray into entrepreneurship, and we did extremely well.

The following stop was the travel agency. I founded a travel agency because I was spending so much money on tours that I couldn't afford to pay my travel agent. I decided to open my own travel agency, Steady State Travel in Mill Valley, and employed the two ladies who had previously worked for the former travel agency. It didn't pay well, but it didn't cost me anything when I went on tour.

Red Rocker Clothing was a flop because the rag trade is the most insane business in the world. I got the brilliant notion of making these fancy flannel shorts. Ralph Lauren sold me the flannel. He had this flannel shirt and stuff line that was the baddest flannel. I probably lost $300,000 because I received a large order from JC Penney's that I couldn't fill. I was running late. Because they wouldn't take them, I ended up with $65,000 worth of flannel shorts in my warehouse. Some of them didn't have buttons because I was rushing them out. Everyone wore flannel shorts the following year. It's a difficult business. You come up with a concept, and the next year everyone rips it off, forcing you to come up with something new. I walked away. While I lost money on the garments, I ended up launching something profitable: bike shops. Bucky was the one who got me interested in motorcycles. Bucky, my old pal who I used to assist steal albums from the ABC Store and who introduced me to Fresh Cream, was living with his wife, Joelle, and their son, Benny, in an apartment on B Street in San Rafael. Bucky eventually got a job at the Corte Madera Cyclery, an old-school Schwinn dealership.

I was making some money from my many enterprises outside of music, so I started buying items. In addition to the house in Marin County, I purchased two others. I became interested in Ferraris. I began to develop an appreciation for great wines. When I was in Montrose, I tasted a 1945 Latour and a 1927 Martinez port on the same night, and I began to collect good wines. As part of my contractual obligations, I required concert producers to give me particular vintage bottles backstage, which I took home unopened. Bill Graham was well aware of my chisel. He had opened all five bottles in my dressing room, preventing me from taking them home, and afterwards gave me a recording machine as a gift. I've only recently begun to live my life. Betsy was also able to spend a lot of money. She was spending money to satisfy herself. She planned to go shopping and redecorate the house. I'd get home and think, "What?" but since I was doing well financially, I didn't mind.

Things were still not going well between us, and I had my first affair around this time. I'd been messing about on the road for years, but this was different. This was a real affair in which I fell in love with someone else. She worked in the music industry. I met her in 1981 while making my debut album with Geffen. She worked for a music publisher and might have a tune for me. She was very self-sufficient.

She was the polar opposite of Betsy: she lived alone, owned her own home, drove a nice car, and worked hard at a good job. I fell in love with her and began a long-term relationship with her. I'd take her on tour via plane. Betsy would leave, and she'd return. I pretended to go to Los Angeles to see her. I was going to fly down for the day. She'd meet me at the airport. We'd go to her house and have some wild sex. She was so free—I adored that about her. My God, this woman can take care of me, I thought.

After two years of the affair, I was ready to leave Betsy, but I decided that we needed to take a family vacation first, this huge trip to Africa. Betsy, Aaron, and I went on safari in Italy, Sardinia, Egypt, and Kenya for six weeks. We were gone for the entire summer of 1983. I was pondering what I was going to do with my girlfriend. I needed to figure out who I was. I had intended to leave Betsy. I was madly in love.

We were on the island of Sardinia. Aaron was at the pool, so Betsy and I had a little afternoon brawl. It was a lovely day, and everything was in order. I knew she was pregnant right away. That had also happened the first time with Aaron. We did it that time while listening to Procol Harum's Salty Dog album on a little record player in a hotel room, and I simply knew. It wasn't spectacular sex or anything in Sardinia—it was more of a quickie deal—but you could tell something happened.

CHAPTER 5

5150

I was cooked crisp when I got off the trip. I shaved off all of my hair. I cancelled the tour's final four gigs after injuring my foot—twisted my ankle in Connecticut and couldn't walk on it. I attempted one such show, failed, and returned home. That year, we performed ninety gigs.

My Ferrari 512, seen in the "I Can't Drive 55" video, was in Claudio Zampolli's store in Van Nuys, where I'd purchased it. He was an Italian mechanic who also worked as a salesman (he's the guy I'm talking to in the "I Can't Drive 55" video). He didn't have a dealership or anything, but he'd purchase you a car. He used to be a test driver for Ferrari. After I ordered the 512, it took nine months to arrive. That year, they made about twelve. Anyway, after I'd had the car for a time, it needed a tune-up, which is a huge, expensive process on these unique cars. It's a true race car, and a tune-up can cost as much as a new car. I returned home without retrieving my car. Claudio also worked on Eddie Van Halen's automobiles, a Lamborghini and a Countach. Eddie noticed my automobile at Claudio's and inquired about it.

"Hey man, nice car," he commented. "Whose car is that?"

"Sammy Hagar," Claudio said. "You should call him up and get him in the band."

Everyone was aware that vocalist David Lee Roth had quit Van Halen a few months before. He left the band nearly as soon as his small solo single, "Just a Gigolo," began to gain traction. It was too soon to say they were in trouble, but their problem was widely known.

"You got his phone number?" Eddie inquired.

The phone rang at my place. Eddie Van Halen was there. "Hey, man, what are you doing?" he inquired.

"I just got back from tour and I'm just kind of nursing my foot," I explained.

"Would you like to get together, come down, and jam," he asked, "and maybe join Van Halen?"

"Not really," I replied. "I'm scorched. I'd be delighted to see you, however..."

I'd only met Eddie a few times before. We'd been to a few major festivals together, and he'd come to my dressing room. "I'm such a big Montrose fan," he'd remarked. "What a nice guy," I thought to myself, "so humble and sweet." When you shook his hand, he always held it with both hands and added a slight bow.

"How about tomorrow?" he proposed.

"No, man, I can't," I responded flatly. "I'm scorched. At least a few days. Allow me to call you back."

We swapped phone numbers and then hung up. I began to think. Maybe if they break up, I can get Eddie to join my band. I could use someone like him. Or maybe I'll just compose some songs with him and have him play on my next album. I was an avid follower. But I despised Dave. He rubbed me the wrong way. I'm sure I irritate a lot of people, so I'm not putting him down. I couldn't tolerate the guy, even if he was a great front man with a great attitude in rock and a hellish image. He was the polar opposite of everything I believed in and who I am. First and foremost, the guy isn't a terrific vocalist, and he behaves like he's the coolest, hottest guy in the world, even though he appears gay to me. He was never convincing to me.

The phone call was not entirely unexpected. Ted Templeman had been the one to inform me that Roth had divorced a few months before, and I'd told Betsy at the time, "They're going to call me, you watch." Who else could they possibly get? Ozzy Osbourne, Ronnie James Dio, and I were there. I was sitting there with goosebumps on my arm when Eddie called. A few days later, I went down to see him. I walked into their Studio City location. Alex Van Halen burst out laughing when he saw my short hair. "You look like somebody put a doughnut on your head and cut it off," he said. I shaved the sides and left a small amount on top. I was going to take a year off. Alex was high on his a$$. He drank a case of tall malt liquor cans every day. He pummelling them as well. He could shotgun like nobody's business. He was continually looking for ways to hold competitions. He'd fall asleep several times a day, wake up, shotgun two or three beers, crack one more, and stroll out of the room. Eddie, too, drank all day. They both awoke, grabbed a beer, and lit a cigarette, and that was how they began their day. They'd slumber at four o'clock in the afternoon. They were both huge nappers.

Eddie shared a modest home with his actress wife, Valerie Bertinelli. It was Valerie's place; Eddie had just moved in with her. She also had a second home in Malibu, a type of beach house, and they shared their time between the two. The major one, however, was located in the hills above Coldwater Canyon. He'd converted an ordinary two-bedroom house with a carport into a studio. They named the studio "5150," after the police code for apprehending a lunatic. It wasn't a rock-star pad, and the studio was a shambles. Engineer Donn Landee had developed a handcrafted board that looked like it came out of a Cracker Jack box. Landee made the board sound amazing, but he was a genius who knew how to use it. To anyone else, it looked like model aeroplane equipment. The studio was disgusting. There were beer cans everywhere, as well as ashtrays full of cigarettes. To connect something into the board, Donn Landee had to blow away the cigarette ashes. The place smelt like the world's worst bar. I doubt it had ever been cleaned. Eddie's guitars were scattered over the floor. Nothing in racks, nothing in cases, just on the floor, on chairs, leaning against amps, against the wall, in a pile in the corner. It was lovely, but I'd never seen anything like it before.

Eddie strolled in, sporting a pair of those sunglasses with louvres. He'd been up all night drinking and trying to compose music. I had no idea who these people were. I had no idea what their regimen was. They were, however, battered. Eddie was dressed in crumpled jeans. I discovered why when I went into their house later that day. Valerie and he were living out of their bags. They'd been off the road for a few months, but their belongings weren't in their closets. It was on the floor in their bags. There were stacks of junk all over the place. It was strange. They could afford maids, but they lacked them. They were children. When you think about it, they had been on the road for five years and had only recently returned home. Eddie never bothered to unpack his belongings. He was constantly pulling garments out, hoping to find something partially clean but wrinkled. All of this struck me as amusing, as if to say, "Far out, these guys really don't care." That was pretty fantastic, in my opinion. I arrived from another realm, Betsy's world. My clothing had been ironed. My socks had been pressed, folded, and stored in the closet. I was dressed like a Miami Vice in an Armani linen jacket and pants, a T-shirt, and tennis shoes. I dined at great restaurants and drank fine wine. Eddie would microwave a frozen hot dog and bun, nuke it, plough it into his mouth, then guzzle it down with a beer. There were some discarded pizza boxes sitting around. The freezer was stocked with frozen burritos.

Al was the insane one. He was loud, inebriated, making comments, laughing at dumb things, and smoking cigarettes. "Here," he'd say, "shotgun this beer." I'm not a beer drinker. They'd been up all night writing when I arrived. They had what would become "Summer Nights" and "Good Enough." Eddie, Al, and Mike Anthony, the bassist, had remained up late jamming. When I arrived at midday, they still hadn't gone to bed. They were also ripped. They'd been drinking the entire time. I went down to see Eddie. In my mind, there was no way I was going to join Van Halen.We began playing, and Donn Landee, the engineer, recorded everything we did. The first sentence was made up on the spot: "Summer nights and my radio." When I initially heard the riff, it just came to me. I scattered my way through the rest of the song. I did the same thing with "Good Enough"—I was really on point. Eddie couldn't believe his eyes. Dave didn't appear to have excellent rhythm and wasn't a terrific singer with a limited range. Eddie and I were singing Eddie's guitar licks together. They were freaking out after five hours.

"We've got a band," they insisted.

"I don't know," I admitted. "That sounds fantastic, but let's talk about it." "Perhaps I'll return next week or something."

They urged me to stay, but I walked home and grabbed a tape. We jammed a blues tune and had the other material that we had worked on. I put the cassette on my stereo after dinner. I had goosebumps all over my body. I was aware of it. It was Cream all over again, my favourite rock band of all time. There was something slow, confident, almost majestic about it. My rock had always been stronger. Even though it was an up-tempo beat, they were relaxed. Alex reclined, as Ginger Baker always did. Eddie played like Clapton, deep in the pocket. He didn't speed anything up. I'd never played with such guys before. I called Ed Leffler and said, "I'm doing it." He told me I was insane. He believed the Van Halens were insane and that I was insane to even consider doing it. He then got right to work. "Let me see what I can do," he offered. Leffler examined their predicament. They were in a terrible financial situation since they had made a lot of money but had squandered it all. They were flying around like crazy. When Leffler found out how much the guys made the previous year, he informed me I'd have to take a salary reduction if I wanted to join the band. But as we started playing the music, I knew everything would fall into place.

EDDY WAS He is a man of few words. His favourite phrase was "Yeah, yeah, yeah." All he cared about was getting some sleep, drinking some beer, smoking some cigarettes, and listening to music. Eddie wasn't a really motivated musician. I became concerned with his nonchalance, his lack of concern for the whole affair, while working on the first record. He wasn't the musical genius who told everyone what to play. Al did what he wanted, and Mike did what he wanted. Eddie had no idea what the lyrics were. He was only concerned with his guitar part. That was all he focused on.

When I created "Love Walks In," his wife, Valerie, was so taken with the music that she forced him to listen to the words. He became overcome with emotion. "Wow, I've never listened to lyrics before," he exclaimed. He couldn't even sing you a single tune. He had no idea what fucking Dave was singing about. He was checking his guitar and the groove to make sure his part was correct.Mike was my Ed McMahon, always ready to support whatever the play was. Eddie and Al were as close as nails. They didn't get too far apart. They passed cigarettes back and forth. One cannot light one without also lighting one for the other. Only one match was required. They never entered the room with only their own beer. They were usually carrying a beer for the other person. It was lovely until they started fighting, at which point it became dreadful. They would fight at least once a week when they were both drinking. I mean, just go for it. Fistfights. Mike and I would try to separate them. We'd break them up and leave, then Al would drive back and they'd fight again. When we arrived at the studio the next day, the windshield had been shattered and the garbage can had been turned over.

Valerie, wow, such a cool lady. I didn't see much of Eddie's wife. When I pulled into the driveway one day, Valerie and Eddie were sipping a beer on the hood of one of Ed's automobiles. That was amazing to me. My wife would never do something like that. Valerie was cool with the guys. She wasn't always present because she was working. She was almost always booked for a little film or television role. She also spent a significant amount of time at their beach cottage. Van Halen had a strong sense of family. Jan, their father, was often drinking and smoking when I first arrived. Mike Anthony was the most devoted canine on the earth. He carried the flag. They trusted me from the outset, and I became the motivator. They adored it and rallied around me. It was incredibly family-like and close. It's just us versus the rest of the world. This is our home. We're working on our album. We didn't fight over nothing. It had all come true.

Even still, there was some scepticism regarding Van Halen. No one seemed to believe in the band's prospects at the moment. Roth had split with the road crew and management, and he appeared to be on his way to stardom on his own, leaving the band in his wake. People suggested naming it Van Hagar, which was a poor idea. (I didn't realise it at the time—Dad always claimed to be Irish—but we were actually Dutch, and our surname may have been Van Hagar once at a time.)

Despite our reservations, we knew it would work because we were the ones in the studio working on the 5150 record and knew we had some outstanding music. We had "Why Can't This Be Love." Nobody except us had heard any of this because we couldn't even tell anyone we were in the studio together. Everything had been done behind closed doors because I was signed to Geffen and Van Halen to Warner Bros. Although we weren't aware of it, Geffen and Warner Bros. were already feuding. Warner Bros., as Geffen's distributor, took 50% of Geffen's earnings at the time, and I was Geffen's biggest artist at the time. Elton John had never worked for Geffen Records. Neil Young was a flop, and Geffen eventually sued him. He didn't have any hits from Donna Summer. There was me, Don Henley, who had one successful album, and John Lennon, who died soon after giving Geffen his first album, despite the fact that it sold millions after he was shot. Geffen was unlikely to allow his biggest star to stroll across the street only to sing with another band. I took Leffler to see David Geffen. He didn't like the idea and tried to talk me out of it, as we expected.

"Why would you want to be in that band?" he wondered. "You're as big as them on your own." He was perplexed. He sat at his desk, his hand on his head. "I don't understand this," he said. He, like many others, thought David Lee Roth would be a difficult act to follow, and he said so.

He abruptly changed his tone after a few minutes of deliberation. "I would never, ever stop an artist from doing what they want to do," he stated. "My name is David Geffen. I advocate for the artist. I support the artist. First and foremost, it is about you and your life." He stated that he would consult with Mo Ostin, the head of Warner Bros. Records. With Warner Bros. over a barrel, Geffen told them he'd let them have me for one record in exchange for a Sammy Hagar solo album right after. He wanted 100% of the solo album and 50% of the Van Halen releases to be distributed by Warner Bros. Mo Ostin, the CEO of Warner Bros., visited Eddie's 5150 Studios to discuss the situation. He was, to put it mildly, wary. He recommended renaming the band, and he loved the Van Hagar idea.Eddie and I debated it and decided, no, we're Van Halen. We adored one another. There was no hostility, no egos, nothing. They wanted me to be a part of this band, and I wanted to be a part of it because we were making music and knew we were fantastic. Mo requested if he could hear something, so we put on our instruments and played "Why Can't This Be Love" for him live and in person while he sat there. He smiled as he waved his finger in the air.

"I smell money," Mo declared.

We were already halfway through the record when Warner Bros. and Geffen gave us the go-ahead. After that, we pushed full throttle, and things began to move quickly. Eddie and Al had a lot of songs left over from what would have been the next Van Halen album if Roth hadn't parted up with them. When I stepped in, they had a bunch of semi-formed ideas. All of the words and melodies had to be written by me. I worked on their jams, picking them apart and turning them into tunes. I was a little behind the times with the lyrics. We'd spend hours jamming in the studio. I'd sing and experiment using a handheld microphone and headphones. When anything was good, I'd instruct the engineer to produce a cassette. When I returned to Malibu, which was approximately an hour away, I would take the cassettes of the bits I wanted to preserve with me. I'd drive home with my ears bleeding and listen to the music. Ed and Al smoked like chimneys in the studio. Those guys would light them up, set one down, light another, and place it in an ashtray. They'd be smoking three or four cigarettes at once. They were chain smokers, lighting one cigarette and leaving the filter burn in the ashtray. Never, ever put them out. Dropping them to the ground. When I got home at three o'clock in the morning and went directly to the shower because I stank like cigarette smoke, I'd get these terrible migraines.

On the way home one night, I was listening to this cassette on which Eddie had written the music and noodled the verses on guitar. He was attempting to demonstrate the phrasing of the verses, but he was unable to do so since he couldn't play the rhythm and the lead at the same time. I didn't understand what he was doing. But, on the way home, I noticed the rhythm and began singing it in the car. We didn't have a chorus, so I just started singing "Best of Both Worlds." It hit me hard as I was turning into the garage. Bang. The chorus was a success. I took a shower, but I kept coming out to dry myself and jot down some more lyrics on a piece of paper. Then I'd hop back in the shower...and then back out to scribble some more. The song washed over me like a flood. I'm not familiar with lyricists. It's the easiest thing in the world, according to lyricist Bernie Taupin. Once he gets a title and a concept, he can simply go bam-bam-bam-bam-bam-bam, and it's done. This song was crashing down on me like a tidal wave. Even taking a shower was impossible for me. I usually get portions that I can recall. I just keep singing them in my brain and then write them down. I created the entire song while still in the shower. The next day, I went in and sang it. Everyone was taken aback. It was the "Best of Both Worlds."

Eddie has never actually performed a proper keyboard ballad in his entire life till I wrote "Love Walks In." The closest Roth came was "Wait" from 1984, which was a synth track but a rocker. It wasn't lovely music. I had been reading Ruth Montgomery's book Aliens Among Us. She claims to be a natural writer. She simply takes a pencil, closes her eyes, and enters a trance, and the writing flows through her. The book was about walk-ins, or aliens who enter your body while you are sleeping. A person cannot die and still become a completely different person. They wake up one morning and have no idea who they are. I wrote about how love may transform you into a whole different person. Eddie and I became the closest collaborators after Valerie compelled Eddie to listen to the lyrics, trusting and loving each other from that moment forward.

Before I joined van halen, I'd committed to farm aid in September 1985, and we agreed it was where we'd make the news. I wanted to go big with this. For our final gig, I booked a private plane for my band. I provided a hefty bonus to everyone. They'd all previously bought houses, but I gave them enough money to pay them off if they wanted. I invited Eddie to join us in rehearsal. While Eddie was in town, Eddie and I wrote three songs in two days. Eddie and I practised Led Zeppelin's "Rock and Roll" for Farm Aid. It was going to be fantastic. Unfortunately, I messed everything up. You could only perform three or four songs at Farm Aid. Willie Nelson, John Cougar Mellencamp, and Neil Young coordinated the twelve-hour marathon fund-raiser, which was broadcast live on radio and television and featured musicians such as Kris Kristofferson and Jimmy Buffett. It wasn't a rock concert. When it was my turn, Dylan was as hard-rocking as it had gotten. I planned to start with "One Way to Rock," then "I Can't Drive 55," then bring out Eddie, announce that I was joining Van Halen, and play "Rock and Roll." I got out and immediately had that stadium rocking. They were crazy in love with me. I was getting points. It was a major deal for me— 90,000 people in Champagne, Illinois, one of my most important regions. I could stay in Chicago for two nights, Champagne for two nights, and Peoria for two nights. My home state was Illinois. I was tearing it up when I took the stage to introduce "I Can't Drive 55."

"Here's a song for all you tractor-pulling motherfuckers," I yelled, and they immediately turned off the radio broadcast and the live TV feed. Everything was damaged by me. We had been off the air for quite some time when I summoned Eddie, and no one had seen or heard anything. He played a brief solo before we made the announcement and began the Led Zeppelin piece. That was our first public performance as a group. Eddie was with us on the plane. We all flew back in good spirits. It was a smooth transition from my previous band to Van Halen.

Many years later, David Lauser attended a cattle-call audition for drummers for Maria McKee, the former vocalist of Lone Justice, the Geffen-signed country-rock band that was scheduled to join us at Farm Aid. They thought they had the Eagles and Linda Ronstadt rolled into one, but Lone Justice was not to be. A few years later, the vocalist was looking for a drummer, and Lauser appeared to be the frontrunner. He's down to the last interview, and she says, "Tell me about yourself—what have you done in the past?" "I've worked for Sammy Hagar my entire life," Lauser says. She stands up and exits the room. I suppose there was still some resentment about that. I had no intention of doing anything improper. I moved into a rented house when I initially came down to join Van Halen, but then a foreclosure came up for sale next door to Eddie and Valerie in Malibu. They lived on a bluff, with a small house in the middle and my house in the middle. It was all brand new, but the contractor went bankrupt, and the bank took over. I received the house despite making an extremely low offer. Eddie and I moved in next door. It was incredible that a place would pop up on Broad Beach Road, one of the most desirable streets in North Malibu, especially at such low prices. It appeared to be karma. Betsy was having a good time. She enjoyed the house and the beach. She wasn't interested in Malibu, but there were horses just down the street. For what we paid for her horses at the Malibu stables, you could rent a villa in the south of France, but she was content. Betsy was thrown into a loop when I joined Van Halen. She'd been waiting for me to slow down and leave the business. She wasn't prepared for me to start anew with a completely different band. But when the house in Malibu came up for sale, she began to reconsider. I went to work every day and came home every night. We were finishing up the album and preparing for the tour. She was residing in this lovely beach mansion. She had roses in her garden and horses down the road. She either drove her new Jaguar or the Land Rover.

Every day, Eddie and I would drive to the studio. He and I had the vehicles. We'd take a Ferrari, a Lamborghini, my E-Jag, or a Cobra. We passed past a dealer one day on our way to the studio and saw an E-Jag sitting there. I came to a halt. I went in, called my business manager, passed the phone to the salesman, and the two of them closed the deal. I went out to my car and drove to the studio. I slid behind the wheel, but wait, what's with the seat? I'm not that huge, but whomever drove this automobile before me was a short guy. Whose vehicle is this? Ronnie James Dio owned it. That was fantastic. Eddie and I did insane things like that. We'd race home at 140, 150 miles per hour, myself in one of my Ferraris and Eddie in one of his Lamborghinis. He was always inebriated. We'd go from two o'clock in the afternoon till past midnight every day, unless Al passed out. Eddie used to nurse his beers while Al was a nasty drunk. He was continually drinking, yet he never got drunk. Al would screw up, puke, and pass out. You'd have to slap him around, give him a couple of hours to relax, pick him up, and bring him back. We'd limit his beer intake, and he'd sneak out for a pack of cigarettes, rush downtown, buy a bottle of vodka, and drink it in the store.

Their father drank as well. Eddie didn't get up at eight o'clock in the morning, so we were at the studio until two o'clock in the afternoon. When I arrived at the studio, the three of them were already drinking, having gone through a couple of six-packs. Jan Van Halen, their father, was a wonderful man. I felt a strong connection to him. He was a saxophonist. He appreciated my skills and the fact that I could sing. Those people, on the other hand, drank. Al, like my father, was an alcoholic. He couldn't stop himself. He drank until he passed out, awoke, and began again. He would approach individuals in pubs and offer them money to light a cigarette on their arm or shave their head while videotaping the entire thing. Completely insane.

They were still laughing at Al's birthday performance when I arrived. According to legend, they all went to a Benihana. He was already inebriated when he arrived. It's his birthday today. He's sipping hot sake, among other things. He jumps up on the table, removes his shirt, and begins dancing straight on the scorching grill. On it, he had just finished cooking dinner. Al takes his pants down to fuck with the other patrons. He trips himself since his pants are about his ankles, and lands on his back on the grill. Ssssss. He is unable to stand. He flips like a prawn. Ssssss. Awww, awww. Ahhh, sssss! He was powerless to act. He was cooking on the grill. They had to remove him and, of course, transport him to the hospital. He was covered in burns. These individuals were wild, high-maintenance, but good-hearted, as Leffler described them. Another day, during the 5150 session, we were waiting for Claudio to return one of my automobiles about 2:00 p.m.

"I bet you I could shotgun ten beers," Al remarked.

He's carrying ten tales of malt liquor. "I'll bet you a thousand bucks," he said. Al is a gambler. On a bet, he once lost his BMW to me. I also made him pay, and I gave it to our tour manager for Christmas. Al was a kind person, but he was a terrible jerk. I wasn't going to bet on him.

"Oh yeah?" he exclaimed. "Keep an eye on this."

Michael Anthony was standing nearby. Al opened them all first and then drained them one at a time, pow, pow, pow, pow. How can you possibly contain that much in your stomach? "Oh no, this day is over," I thought. Al stepped out into the driveway with a huge belch and a broomstick. "My dad used to do this," he explained. "Have you ever seen anyone do this?"

He was standing on the driveway asphalt, holding the broomstick in front of him with both hands. "What the fuck's he doing?" I pondered as I glanced at him. He's going to leap over the broomstick while holding it. Claudio pulled around the corner in my automobile at that precise moment. Al leapt over the fucking thing, grabbed his feet, of course—drunk, having shotgunned ten cans of malt liquor—and went down, face-first. He refused to let go of the broomstick. We had to take the broom away from him. He landed facedown on the ground and passed out. Claudio screamed as he leaped out of the car. "Call an ambulance," he instructed. "Oh, my God, he's dead."

He did strike hard. The force of his attempt slammed his head against the asphalt. He had a pizza face when we picked him up. He was taken away in an ambulance. I went home, took the next day off, and returned the next day. Al was curled up on the couch, his head covered like a mummy's. I laughed so hard at him, but he couldn't laugh, which only made it worse. He actually caused a lot of harm to his face. That was just getting started on the record. You could only guess what the tour would be like. We needed a new producer when it came time to record the album because Ted Templeman, who was producing David Lee Roth's solo records, had allegedly been bad-rapping us to Warner Bros. behind our backs, so we weren't going to work with him. Despite Mo Ostin's happy reaction when he heard us· at 5150, and the fact that they weren't paying much for it, Warner Bros. wasn't overjoyed with the proposal. Mick Jones of Foreigner was suggested by me. I'd known him since he was still with Spooky Tooth in Montrose. So Mick joined us and co-produced the CD.

Mick and I were walking on the beach one day at the end of the project when he turned to me and asked, "Give me one more song." That was the song "Dreams." He just sort of drew it from me. I had no idea what key the song was in. I began singing in that range. Mick became enthralled and assisted me in learning to sing in this hitherto unseen supersonic range. He forced me to sing an octave higher than I typically would. Mick had me do things I had never idea I could do.

We cut the record in less than a month, but we got stuck mixing. It took longer to mix than we planned because Eddie's studio was not conducive to mixing. We'd make the mixes, take them home, and not like what we heard, so we'd have to start over. We had to cancel events in Alaska and Hawaii at the outset of the tour. We wanted to start in a secluded location because we were concerned about how people would react to the new material.

There was also the Van Halen catalogue issue. I informed the guys that I did not want to be a part of a cover band. I wasn't going to do any shows until we had an album, and even then, I didn't want to play too much old crap. They were completely on board with it. We all decided to go out and protest. In the end, we were so late with the tapes that the record couldn't be released until a week after the tour's first scheduled date. Rather than starting somewhere far away, we started it all in Shreveport, Louisiana. We went on with the show despite the fact that the record was late because it had already sold out and we didn't want to cancel or postpone it. People had heard the single "Why Can't This Be Love" on the radio, so they had heard something, but they hadn't heard the album.

On March 27, 1987, we went to Shreveport, Louisiana, for our first gig, and I was a wreck. I'm not sure I've ever been more nervous before a performance. We took the stage and began with "One Way to Rock," one of my compositions. The barricade was destroyed. The audience erupted. It happened in an instant, like a flash of lightning. It was lethal. At that moment, we realised we were on top of the world. The irony is that that day had been predicted a few years before by a clairvoyant named Marshall Lever. I met him through an acupuncturist and went to see him at his house in Sausalito for an appointment somewhere during the recording of VOA. This was after I had broken up with the girlfriend and was enjoying my new son, Andrew, but I still had a feeling something wasn't quite right between Betsy and me. I felt compelled to speak with someone. I needed spiritual guidance. His wife greeted me, a red-lipped, silly woman who led me inside the room. This large man entered, sat in a rocking rocker, leaned back, and closed his eyes. His wife asked if I wanted to record the session and inserted a tape into a tape recorder. His dog followed them inside the room, sat on the floor, and began to snore. I'd seen this person twenty times throughout the years, and this was the pattern. Every one of my tapes has that dog snoring.

He began by informing me that I was in a relationship that I was about to end. "She was your sister in a past life in Greece," he explained. "You were separated when she was nine years old and you were eleven years old, and your parents were killed in a boating accident in the Greek islands." They committed her to a convent, and you left on a fishing boat and never returned. You never saw her again, and you regretted it. When you saw her and smelled her"— he's talking about the smell, this lady drove me crazy with her smell—"when you smelled her, you recognized who she was and you didn't want to be away from her again."

He then told me about Betsy. "Betsy was also your sister in a past life," he explained, "and you lived in Spain." Neither of you have ever married. You were in love, but you never had sex because she was your sister and you had spent your entire life together. Betsy was your older sibling. Your mother passed away while giving birth to you. Betsy cooked for you, exactly like your wife, but even though you were madly in love, you never had sex. Crulli, C-R-U-L-L-I, you were a producer of instruments." He stated it clearly. "And your instruments can be seen in a museum in Barcelona."

He focused his attention on Betsy. "When you met your current wife, you had an extremely strong sexual relationship, and it's really what keeps you tied," he explained. That's exactly what we had. Even after twenty years, our sexual relationship was amazing. How did he find out all of this?

"In eighteen months," he added, "you'll embark on a brand-new adventure, similar to what you're doing now, but different." More strong, bigger, and eerily similar to 'this is it.'"

That's when he told me about the date. He stated that it would begin on that date. I declined to perform "Jump." It was just difficult for me. I compose my own music. Lyrically, "Jump" was difficult for me—"Can't you see me standing here, I've got my back against the record machine, you know what I mean?" "I may as well jump." That was difficult for me. I couldn't sing the song with any feeling or passion. I have to sing something meaningful.

"Hey, hey, hey you, who were you?" "How have you been, baby?" I just couldn't sing that garbage, no matter how good it was. In a panic the first night, I dragged a guy from the audience to sing it. The audience erupted. The band felt it was fantastic. When he said, "I might as well," I'd leap into the air like a lunatic. It was successful. We decided to keep it. I only sang "Jump" twice during the entire tour.

Van Halen didn't have a particularly tight concert before I joined the band. Roth was a talker. They'd perform another tune. Ed would do a 20-minute guitar solo. They were going to perform another tune. Roth would continue to speak, another song would be played, then Al would have a thirty-minute drum solo. They told me on the 1984 Tour that they would perform eight songs in a two-hour set. And they all ended the same way. They finished with a classic heavy-metal crescendo—four crashes...One, two, and three. Al would generally do something at the end of that, smack this, clang that, simply because he was odd. I decided we needed a fresh start.

"Great idea," Eddie remarked, as he always does. So, while pounding beers, Al discovered a fresh ending. Good. The next day during rehearsal, it was back to the same old ending. If he learned anything, it was only for one day. Nothing stayed. On the tour, we preserved the same finale. On the road, the crew worked carefully around Al, attempting to figure out how he wouldn't pass out during the event. Al would sleep right up to the moment we went onstage. I'd walk into the dressing room from the hotel—I never did sound checks to save my voice—and find the two of them sleeping on the couch or on a chair. They never returned to the motel for a snooze. Everyone walked on tiptoes around them.

"Shhh, let them sleep," they'd advise. "Don't wake them up, or Al will start drinking way too soon."

They'd wake Al up approximately twenty minutes before the show. There was usually a supply of tall Schlitz cans on hand. He would down three or four drinks and get high. He'd stroll on onstage with a couple more cans in his hands, pound them, and drink the rest of the case throughout the course of the two-hour performance. During the show, the crew would set out these large rubber garbage cans for him to piss in. He'd piss in the trash can after almost every song, pound a couple of drinks, and then start playing again. He'd become extremely messed up at times. He'd get up from the drums in the middle of a song to pee or gulp a beer. He eventually started wearing one of those helmets with drink holders and straws on the side. He needed assistance near the end of the tour. This was the heyday of arena rock. I'd been working in arenas and Standing Hampton since 1982. I grew up listening to arena rock. Montrose made venues available to everyone. I never performed in nightclubs or theatres. I'd have no idea what it was like. I was used to going out with the huge movements, stretching my hands as far as they could go, rushing across the stage, jumping as high as I could to get to those folks at the back of the massive venues.

Van Halen was the archetypal arena-rock outfit. Arenas had vanished by the conclusion of our journey. People began to perform in amphitheatres for greater money. Arenas were more expensive and smaller. A large production could not be staged in the amphitheatres. When we first began performing arenas, Ed Leffler and I devised a method to expedite production and stage design in order to sell an additional two thousand seats in the rear, behind the stage. Those seats were all about profit. We did not place a canopy over the illumination so that people could view the stage. We activated the PA system. We learnt all of the tricks and came up with a couple of our own. We made more money than the other bands when we were rushing through arenas after VOA because they weren't selling those last 250 tickets. When I first joined Van Halen, they were draping off the rear of the hall, halving their capacity and going away with a few thousand dollars. We designed the stage for the 5150 Tour so that we could be visible from every angle.

The arenas were enormous and majestic, with roofs that extended all the way to the rear. You might have as many as fourteen spotlights and extend your production as far back as you wished. It was big-time rock when you came out. It was quite noisy. It was within a building, and sound did not simply disappear as it does outside. The hall held the noise. The audience felt it in their chests because it was enormous and thunderous. You could darken the entire structure before slamming these four little guys up there with four big spotlights each. Rock stars became rock gods through arena rock.

We built this massive stage for the 5150 Tour out of steel gratings that led up to another stage about eight feet taller and all the way to the back. That way, I'd be able to work the audience in the rear. We had an eight-foot raise, which was like another stage, where the drum riser was. I'd go up there, and Eddie's go up there. Mike was going to go up there. You may be closer to the back row than the front row, even exchanging high fives with the audience.

On each side, we had two more platforms. Our stage was enormous. We had these light trusses with catwalks that I had been using since the Three Lock Box Tour. At one point during the event, it fell like an X across the front of the stage, and I went up there and out over the audience twenty or thirty feet above their heads. The show was transported in fifteen trucks, with a massive amount of production, some special effects, but largely sound, staging, and lighting.

I was one of the first to use the headset microphone, which allowed me to move about freely. We were all on the internet. We used to walk out onto this big stage and not see each other for five minutes.

Eddie would be running in one direction. Mikey would take off in another direction, and I would be somewhere else. Only Al was trapped where he was. I'd sometimes put my palm over my eyes to see where Eddie was on stage. The stage was spotless save for the big amps since we kept our monitors hidden behind grating on the stage. They were also really noisy. You'd better hold your ear if you went in front of any of the amps. Van Halen turned up the volume. The PA had to be loud since the sound was coming off the stage so loudly. That was arena rock, with bands like Led Zeppelin, Black Sabbath, Deep Purple, Rush, and Van Halen. Stars of rock.

On the tour, there was a former Playboy bunny from California who had seen one of the other men in my old band. Despite the fact that she had always been following me, she managed to hook up with Leffler. She was attractive, but there was something about her that made me suspicious. She discovered my name on Leffler's rooming list and came knocking on my door in Detroit in the middle of the night. I answered the door naked—I slept naked—and she pushed the door open, threw me on the bed, and began blowing on me. That's a difficult thing to get up and walk away from. "Son of a bitch," I thought to myself, "I'm fucked now." And, indeed, I was. Leffler receives the phone call about 10 days later. She's expecting a child. I detected a set-up. I was really enraged. Betsy would kill herself. We hired an attorney and began negotiating with her. I knew it wasn't my child. Extortion was involved.

She wanted a New York apartment and anything else that my children would have. I didn't want to pay anything, but Leffler persuaded me that it was best to give her the money until the baby was delivered and then see what occurred. When she had the kid, she was living in the flat with her boyfriend, a musician in New York. She dialled Leffler's number from the hospital. "Tell Sammy to call me," she instructed. I didn't want to talk to her, but Leffler persuaded me. She tells me the baby is adorable, looks exactly like me, she's madly in love with me, she's very sorry, and other such nonsense. Leffler receives another call a few days later. The infant perished. I don't think she ever had a child. She may have had an abortion at a young age. Marshall Lever, my psychic with the sleeping dog, informed me of the situation. "It's not your baby," he pointed out. "She lives in New York with her boyfriend." She has a musician boyfriend, and this is most likely an extortion case. Don't worry, just relax, and everything will be OK once she has the kid."

I never heard anything else from her. They obviously realised it wasn't my baby. They just kept extorting me for as long as they could. She was never seen again. We were in Atlanta three weeks into the tour when Ed Leffler called a meeting.

"Billboard, number one," he announced.

It was one of us's first number-one hits. The record sold 600,000 copies in its first week and another 400,000 the following week. It was ablaze. It became platinum faster than any other Warner Bros. record in history. Every single one of our albums did. Van Halen was a massive, quick seller when I was in the band. Every album debuted at number one. It was an unfathomably long run.

CHAPTER 6

MONSTERS OF ROCK

I had to do the solo record for Geffen as soon as we ended the first tour. That was the agreement he'd reached with Warner Bros. We were concerned about Eddie and his drinking and drug addiction, but we had to deal with his brother first. As soon as the tour ended, we put Al in rehab. His wife staged a protest. I had no idea what an intervention was. It was a tense situation. I sobbed. It shattered me, and I wasn't even the one with the gun. They went and got him out of bed around six a.m., before he had another drink. He was getting out of bed at four a.m., chugging a bottle of vodka, and returning to bed. He was not a drinker. He didn't work as a nurse. He simply ploughed himself till he passed out. We admitted him to the hospital. He took the pledge and vowed never to drink again. I adore Al. He is the strongest, yet strange. He's a chain smoker, but he'd quit smoking for one day every Monday just to torture himself. Al is the type of guy I'd call every day just to BS.

Eddie had no one to drink with after All cleaned up. Al continued to smoke. Eddie would drink beer and do a few other things while Al drank coffee. Eddie co-produced and played bass on my solo album, which was Leffler's idea. He always played bass with Van Halen, on two or three songs on almost every album. He was a fantastic bassist. Eddie is a fantastic musician in general.

So we proceeded into the studio, where we were joined by Jesse Harms on keyboards, David Lauser on drums, and Eddie on bass. I used to play the guitar. We'd keep Eddie occupied that way. We made the record in A&M Records' brand-new Hollywood facilities, where Tom Petty, John Cougar Mellencamp, and Stevie Nicks had previously worked. Pink Floyd was performing "Learning to Fly" in the room next door without Roger Waters. Every day, Eddie and I would take a different automobile back from the beach. Down there,

I had approximately seven Ferraris. Nick Mason, the drummer for Pink Floyd, is an avid Ferrari collector. Although guitarist David Gilmore has Ferraris, he is not in Nick Mason's league as a collector. Mason has one of the first Ferrari GTOs, which is likely worth $30 million. They didn't have their cars with them, so they'd stand on the sidewalk every day to watch what I'd be driving. David Gilmore is one of my all-time guitar heroes, and having those men admire my cars every day was extremely nice. I was bragging. I sent Bucky backup to Mill Valley to change out a couple more cars after I'd gone through all of the automobiles I had down south.

Pink Floyd was auditioning drummers for a shuffle they couldn't nail, even with their drummer Nick Mason there. They had Omar Hakim trying out, fresh from Sting's band, but they didn't use him on the track. I did. He overdubbed drums on a couple cuts on my album. Pink Floyd was so particular about that shuffle, they were still working on it by the time I finished my entire album.

MTV did a whole "Name the Album" promotion, because I couldn't go on tour. I was just going to call it Sammy Hagar, but some fan submitted the title I Never Said Goodbye, with a note saying, "Sammy's left his solo career but he never said goodbye." The record went platinum immediately. "Give to Live" and "Eagles Fly" off the album were big hits. I did a three-week promotional tour around the world—from San Francisco to Japan to Germany, came home and went straight into the studio to start the new Van Halen album, OU812.

As soon as I came back home, I flew down to Los Angeles from San Francisco. Eddie and Al met me at the airport. I hadn't seen them for a couple of weeks. I was really happy to see them. When we got in the car, Eddie and Al lit up cigarettes in the front seat and snapped a cassette in the player.

"We want you to hear something," Eddie said. They played me the keyboard part for "When It's Love." I was covered in goosebumps.

That was almost the inspiration for the whole album. We knocked that song out and knew we had something.

The songs were not my best stuff lyrically. "Black and Blue" was kind of quirky, cool groove and phrasing, but the lyrics were a little too eighties. "Source of Infection," ugh. The last song we wrote was "Finish What Ya Started." It was toward the end of the project and we needed another song or two. Ed was the best at taking an idea you gave him and turning it into something special, something unique. I told him we should do something like the Who's "Magic Bus," something with a lot of rhythm and acoustic guitars. Van Halen hadn't really done anything with acoustic guitars. I was in Malibu, lying in bed with my wife, about to get some, when I heard Eddie outside my door. Not even my front door, but the beach entrance directly under my bedroom deck. I could see him out there, cigarette glowing in the dark, no shirt, acoustic guitar around his neck, bottle of Jack Daniel's in his hand.

"Ed, what?" I said.

"Come on, man. I've got this idea," he said.

"Ed, it's two o'clock in the morning," I said. "I'm tired."

"The old lady kicked me out," he said. "Come on, man. Let me in."

I went down. Betsy was pissed, but what could I do? He was my best friend and creative partner. She turned out the light. I wouldn't let him in, because he's got his cigarette, so we sat on the porch. He started playing me the riff for "Finish What Ya Started" and right away, I got excited. I went and got my acoustic and started doing my Tony Joe White thing. I was still thinking about going back upstairs and getting laid and started singing, "Come on, baby, finish what you started." It never happened. Eddie and I saw the sun come up and I

47

threw him out, but we had written just about the whole thing. I was imagining what was going to happen to me when I went back upstairs. That song is about unfulfilled sex.

It took a while to do OU812, more than it probably should have. Sober, Al played differently. It was really weird. He wasn't as good. When he was drinking, Al was always a radical drummer. He'd hit hard and do crazy fills. Drunk, he was off the hook, but sober, he was a lot more conservative. His timing was better, but he wasn't as radical. In the end, it was easy to put aside things like that, because everybody was still getting along really well. The only problem was that I was starting to burn out, getting a little crispy around the edges. Betsy, on the other hand, was losing it. I'd come off the VOA Tour, jumped into 5150, did the album and the tour, did my solo record, went around the world on the promotional tour, and straight back into the studio for OU812. And now we were going back on the road. She was crying, depressed all the time. Life was not good at home. I was not ignoring it any longer. Now I was concerned. I approached Ed Leffler and offered that we do stadiums. We were in the biggest band in the world, and we were selling out arenas all over the world four nights a week. Stadiums would allow us to go out for a few months rather than a year, and if everything went well, we'd wind up generating a lot more money. Leffler thought it was a risk worth taking.

We drafted legislation. Kingdom Come was a new German band that everyone expected to be big. The Germans sounded just like Led Zeppelin, but they claimed they'd never heard of them. So they were history before they even got out of the starting blocks. They did, however, open. Metallica, who came on second, was my choice. They were a new Bay Area band, youthful and hip. Dokken, the third act, were on the verge of breaking up when the tour began, and following Metallica every night finished them out. They disbanded at the end of the tour. The Scorpions were also on that tour, which meant a lot to me. Between Memorial Day and the end of July 1988, we called the tour Monsters of Rock and played twenty-seven performances. We had 56 trucks, three entire stages, and production equipment to set up all at once so that we could go out and do three gigs a week. Each show cost $350,000, and it was easy to lose money. The performances broke even at 44,000 tickets, yet the tickets were pricey.

However, the fact that OU812 went straight to number one made it simpler to sell tickets. It sold 4 million albums and included the big successes "When It's Love" and "Finish What Ya Started." Meanwhile, that tour made a lot of money, despite not doing so well in some regions. Two Detroits were completely sold out. We ran out of Texxas Jams. Candlestick Park in San Francisco was completely sold out. We sold out of two New York homes. However, in Miami, we performed for perhaps 25,000 people before a hurricane blew in and ripped the performance to shreds. We had to come to a halt in the midst. A significant setback. We took it to a few more areas where it didn't fare so well, and we ended up handing a lot of money back to the promoters. It wasn't a flop, far from it, but it wasn't the home run we were hoping for.

I tripped over a metal step during the first song on opening night. Everything was running late, and we hadn't done a full production run-through the day before, as we usually do. The stage was barely finished in time for us to perform on it. I had no idea what was going on. I tripped and crashed on my tailbone, spending the entire night in the hospital after the first show. For my damaged tailbone, I was receiving steroids injected into my ass every day. I was having massages and sitting on ice packs. A grapefruit was stuck to my lower vertebrae.I flew home on my days off to see my doctor. I hobbled into the waiting area on one of those excursions back and there was Miles Davis sitting in a chair. Sting and his wife, Trudy, emerged as the doctor opened the door. "Look. "It's Sammy Hagar," Sting announced. "Sammy, have you met Miles?" the doctor asked as they walked away.

Miles Davis, dressed like a woman in his flashy, badass attire, with skinny cornrows in his hair. Miles extends his hand without standing, and as I reach out to shake his hand, he wraps his other hand around my forearm and lifts himself to his feet. He's using me to help him get out of the chair. I almost died with him. I was suffering from an ear infection. I was suffering from a sinus infection. My tailbone was fractured. Because of my sinusitis, I couldn't sing the entire tour. Every night, I was unable to sing. Because it was so expensive, it was too big of a deal to cancel. We arrived in Texas and I couldn't sing in front of 60,000 people at the Cotton Bowl. I was on the verge of crying on stage. Texas was my home. Texas belonged to me. Long before Van Halen, I was a headliner there. I came to a halt in the middle of the first song.

"I can't sing," I admitted. "I promise you, Van Halen will come back and do a free concert in Dallas."

After we cut the show short, the brothers went nuclear on me. For that, they crucified me. It took three years for us to make amends. We'd had an opening band called Krokus earlier that day at the Cotton Bowl, who were managed by Butch Stone, a Southerner I knew from Montrose days when he managed Black Oak Arkansas. They had planned to broadcast their set live on the radio, but Ed Leffler called it off. Butch was agitated. There was a scream-fest. Someone jumped Leffler in the elevator after the bar closed that night and beat the snot out of him, knocking out a couple teeth, breaking several ribs, and really busting Ed up. He was in the hospital for two weeks.

Still, we moved forward. I told Betsy I was just going away for a month, but when we returned, Leffler began talking about returning to the other markets. The band put me in the backseat of a car returning from a press event—Ed and I were drinking and using coke—and began drilling on me. Al couldn't sit around the house all day now that he was sober.

"I need a life," he said.

Eddie enjoyed being on the road as well. If he and his brother could, they would have played seven nights a week. They were putting a lot of pressure on me.

"I just can't do it," I admitted. "I love you guys, but I'm going to divorce." My family will be taken away from me. It's not worth it for me." We weren't fighting, but we were arguing.

"We got you in the band, and we thought you were committed," Alex explained. "If we had known this, we would have hired someone else."

Alex was a headtripper when he was sober. He was drunk and tripped out. Eddie would always be there for him, no matter what. In a million years, you couldn't get between the two boys. They're more than simply brothers. They were close because they came from another nation and didn't know English when they arrived. They'd fight like cats and dogs if you got in between them.

The brothers concluded that Mike Anthony wasn't contributing enough to keep his full part of the music publishing. Mikey did not, in fact, write. Ever. He basically did on bass what Eddie told him to do. He was a keen scholar who added to what he was given. Mike was an inventive bassist. He had an excellent background voice that made a significant difference in Van Halen's sound. However, the brothers required funds.

Al was virtually bankrupt. We were making a lot of money, but Al was deeply in debt. Leffler assisted him in consolidating his bills and arranging a five-year window with him only paying interest. He experienced a minor real estate crash. He'd bought a $2 million property, sunk even more money into it for rock-star stuff like a rubber room, and then sold it for a large loss. He was making terrible deals.

We had a meeting and voted to reduce Mike's partnership to 10%. Mikey agreed with the Van Halens and voted against himself, 3-2. Leffler and I voted no.

"I understand what you're saying," he said, "and I'm okay with it."

I knew I'd have to go back out. We spent the fall of 1988 travelling. We didn't have as strenuous a tour. We returned to several of the marketplaces that had been cancelled. We proceeded to some of the secondary markets we had skipped, hoping to keep the record alive and make up for the negative news generated by the Monsters Tour. Everyone believed it was a flop. It didn't work. We made a lot of money and provided for everyone. Nobody lost any money. However, attendance was lower than expected.

We were also doing everything we could to boost album sales, which were excellent but not what they should have been. As a result, we began producing music videos. Van Halen did not create any videos for 5150. Ed Leffler decided not to compete with classic Van Halen videos. Furthermore, Warner Bros. declined to pay for the videos, which might be costly. Warner began to panic when we released the first single from OU812, "When It's Love," without a video as well. They believed that if we had released a video with 5150, we would have sold 10 million instead of 7 million. When the second OU812 single, "When It's Love," came out, we were already on tour, and Warner eventually agreed to pay for a video. Leffler was adamant that it be a performance video. There will be no acting. It had to be shot on one of our days off from the tour.

They dispatched the Warner jet and flew us to Hollywood. We spent twelve hours filming the video, and I completely lost my voice. They loaded us back onto the jet at two a.m. and flew us to the next destination on the tour. They'd shot some B-roll with an actor and actress, and she was there for the shoot, wiping down the bar in the background or something. We had a great connection, but I never got the chance to take her in the back room all day.

The second video, "Finish What Ya Started," was directed by Andy Morahan, who intended to shoot everyone separately. He wanted to make sure everyone looked fantastic all the time, which is impossible to do with four guys at once. Someone is constantly caught with his eyes crossed, a finger in his nose, and his chin doubled. Leffler insisted on a new performance video. They photographed us in black-and-white on a white backdrop. We each spent around three hours playing the tune. When we came in, there were so many racks of clothes that it looked like the men's department at Macy's. We dressed the way we did. We did not allow the stylists to touch our hair or cosmetics. A lady applied a little powder and that was it. We used to watch MTV and giggle at all the dolled-up, blow-dried bands. That was not going to happen.

WE went and did the extra four months of show, but by the time I returned home, my marriage was dying. Betsy had a distant look in her eye. I began to be concerned about her. Al's marriage was also in shambles, and the four months on the road didn't help matters. They were fighting like hell with Al sober and Eddie still fucked up all the time. We were always breaking up conflicts. Over little matters.

"Hey, Ed, have you got a cigarette?"

"Hey, Al, why don't you go out and buy your own fucking cigarettes?"

"Hey, fuck you, man."

"Well, then, fuck you."

Boom. They'd just fight because he requested a smoke. They were usually tense with one other. They would shout at each other in Dutch when they didn't want us to know what they were arguing over. On the second trip, we did not sell out everywhere. We still did a lot of business, but instead of two or three sold-out evenings, we were doing eight thousand out of twelve thousand seats and twelve thousand out of fifteen thousand. Some cities had it all the time, while others required more effort.

Even though the OU812 album sold 4 million copies, people considered it a failure because 5150 had sold 7 million copies, nearly twice as many. Perhaps the honeymoon period is over. There is a lot of strain on me right now. Now we have to make a terrific record and tour the rest of the world. We hadn't yet travelled around the world. I was putting up a fight. I didn't want to leave. Betsy had a nervous breakdown at that point. It all started when I bought this plane, a Merlin 3, and began spending a lot of time in Mexico. We had flown it a few times before I decided to purchase it: a seven-passenger twin turboprop, tiny and fast, the largest plane that can be flown by one pilot. Buying this plane was a bit of a stretch for me. I could afford it, but it was a significant luxury for me. I completely redone the interior with white and beige, cream-coloured leather and suede. I installed a flushing toilet. So the kids could sleep, I had a seat that folded down into a double bed.

Betsy was terrified on our first flight to Mexico on the new plane. When we arrived, she seemed tense. She couldn't sleep and began shaking, suffering from severe anxiety and panic episodes. Bucky's ex-wife, Joelle, was with us; they were divorced at the time. Bucky was living with their son, Benny, and Joelle was working as a nanny for us. We had to leave Mexico because Betsy was in such bad shape. We boarded the plane. We were travelling at 26,000 feet, halfway up the centre of Baja, when she began screaming and tearing her hair out. She attempted to open the door and exit the plane. Aaron was not among us. Andrew was one of them. He was about two years old and asleep. Joelle had me restrain Betsy as I yelled for the pilot to land. He warned me not to land in the middle of nowhere in Mexico with a crazy woman on board. "You've got to let me try to get to San Diego," he insisted. I had some alcohol on the plane, and Betsy was willing to consume it at this point. She never drank or used drugs, but she was so terrified she couldn't breathe. While Joelle held the baby's ears, I poured tequila down her mouth.

Betsy finally relaxed. She collapsed. She was inebriated. When we arrived in San Diego, I arranged for a car to take her to Malibu. We were on our way back to San Francisco, but we had a house in Malibu. I took Andrew on the aircraft, and she and Joelle took the limo to Malibu. Joelle was a close friend of hers. She genuinely looked after her. Betsy was in horrible shape by the time she returned to Malibu. I summoned the doctor, who arrived promptly. He gave her shots that made her feel better. He informed me that she was suffering a panic attack. I'd never heard of a panic attack before. A psychiatrist resided directly across the street. He began spending an hour or two each day at our place. He put her on Prozac, Xanax, and every other antidepressant and mood-enhancing medication available. Betsy had never used drugs before. I had nurses available 24 hours a day, seven days a week. I couldn't abandon her. I couldn't even go to the supermarket. If I told her I was going shopping, she would collapse on the floor and curl up in a ball. I was the only person who could break her trances. We'd try to pry her open, lift her off the floor, and place her on the couch. Her pupils would dilate and she would look blankly ahead. Nobody else could persuade her otherwise. I had to be present. I had a meeting with the Van Halen guys. I told them I couldn't enter the studio. I'm unable to go on tour. I need to get my wife well.

Between the OU812 Tour and For Unlawful Carnal Knowledge, we took a year off. Ed Leffler and I both agreed that a break was necessary for a band that had been in everyone's face for so long. Everyone in the business of making money off of you will advise you to stay out there while you're on top. They say the public forgets quickly.

They are not. Every time they perform, the Stones demonstrate this. Pink Floyd waited as long as they wanted to return to the stage. The bands that tour, tour, tour are the ones who fail. After seeing them twenty times in the last two years, no one wants to see them anymore. Eddie disliked being at home and doing nothing. Every night and every day, I kept an eye on Betsy. Ed and Al were putting a lot of pressure on me. They'd be writing and come up with something interesting, like "Poundcake." When I heard what they were doing, I wanted to be a part of it. I'd come in for a couple of days. We eventually went into the studio to record For Unlawful Carnal Knowledge. We wanted the sound of Led Zeppelin, so we enlisted the help of Andy Johns, the British engineer who worked on the original Led Zeppelin recordings. Too bad he was so messed up. Most of the time, he and Eddie were messed up. We'd start at noon because I needed to be home by dinnertime to assist Betsy.

It was like pulling teeth to make that album. Betsy was in 24-hour care, and the atmosphere at home was difficult. I was trying to prolong the procedure, not because I was lazy. I wanted the album to be fantastic, and I wanted to be there as much as I could, but with all of my troubles at home, there were days when I couldn't go to the studio. Eddie and Al were present at all hours of the day and night. They started pounding me about not being present. "We need you— when are you going to be able to come in?" Eddie would call. I'd come in for a few days, sometimes a week, and occasionally I couldn't come at all. I would bring music home and listen to it. But it's difficult to concentrate while your wife is crying in a ball on the floor. Andy Johns was a shambles, but Eddie shielded him. Eddie needed a new partner in crime now that Al was sober, and Andy fit the bill. A lot of the time, he was bombarded. He slammed into the studio wall with his automobile. I was dissatisfied with the scenario. There was some anxiety in the air. Andy then deleted one of my vocals. That was the end of it. I was no longer working with him. I stormed out of the recording studio.

"Samster, come on, mate," Andy encouraged. "Just one more time."

"Fuck you, Andy, that's the end of it," I said. "I'm done with your ass."

It was difficult to get a vocal with him because he was so disruptive and disinterested. I fired Andy Johns and called back Ted Templeman, who not only produced Montrose and my VOA album, but also handled Van Halen's early albums when Roth was still in the band. Eddie and Ted didn't get along, and Ted had slandered us when we first established ourselves before 5150. Still, Ted came in and sang all of the vocals on For Unlawful Carnal Knowledge alongside me, as well as helped with the mix. He came through for me. I came up with the title. Around this time, the Florida rap group 2 Live Crew brought up the subject of censorship in the music industry. People kept asking us to speak up. To avoid getting too political, I suggested that the following record be titled Fuck Censorship. Leffler anticipated that chain stores would refuse to stock a record with that title. Van Halen, the world's biggest band? Every number one album? They'll do something, shove it in a brown paper bag, anything, anything. They'll figure out a way to sell the record, they're greedy jerks.

Ray "Boom Boom" Mancini, the former lightweight champion, was training me at the time. He came over a couple of times a week and strapped a hundred-pound bag of sand to my back and forced me to run up and down the 77 steps that led down to the ocean from my house. I was showing him some of the material when he inquired about the album's title. "Fuck Censorship," I retorted.

"Oh, wow, man," he exclaimed. "For Unlawful Carnal Knowledge."

I'd never heard that before, so he explained that when a lady was discovered cheating in mediaeval times, she was locked up in the town square and hung a sign around her neck that said "F.U.C.K."—"For Unlawful Carnal Knowledge."

"My mom told me that when I was in school," he explained. "First time I said 'fuck.'"

"Pound Cake," the album's first single, had a fantastic video that reached number one on MTV and was named Rock Video of the Year by Playboy magazine in 1991. We spent roughly $400,000 on that video, which featured a slew of stunning ladies. That was the height of MTV and the music video form, and people were willing to pay for them. When I first saw the treatment for the video for "Right Now," the album's next single, I felt it was a bad idea. That was my first real lyric for Van Halen, and it made a tremendous statement. All I could see were some of the director's lines, such as "I'll wrestle you for food" or "Right now, someone's walking on a nude beach for the first time." I read his treatment and believed he was insane before viewing the video. This song was my child. For six months, I went around in circles with Eddie and Al on this. It was the final track we recorded for the album.

I had these lyrics, but Eddie didn't understand what I was saying and didn't have any music that worked. For months, I had been pounding these men while we were playing video games or eating—"Right now, it's your tomorrow...It's everything right now," but no one was getting it. During a pause, I overheard Eddie playing the piano in the other room. I dashed inside.

"That's it, that's it," I concluded.

"I played this for you on the last album, and you didn't dig it," Eddie explained.

It was a perfect fit. He had no need to modify anything. It would never have occurred if Eddie had gone off and played video games instead, or if I had sat down and began making phone calls like I typically did on breaks. I had a strong attachment to the song. I didn't want to make a stupid video. The Warner Bros. executives found me in Hawaii. They were making every effort to persuade me. Okay, I said, but let me and Al come up with the script. This director included shots in his treatment of me looking in a mirror with an old Van Halen poster in it, with the caption, "Right now, Dave wishes he was Sammy." We began writing together and came up with some fairly amazing lines. I was still not convinced, but I began to sense a spark of interest.

However, when it came time to shoot, we were in Chicago in the thick of winter, trapped inside a blizzard. I was sick with pneumonia and had to cancel two shows. I'd been stuck in a hotel room for days, unwell, grumpy, and irritated. The director was so imprecise with us—"Just stand over here"—that I didn't understand what he was doing. There's a scene at the end where I'm folding my arms and standing there appearing disgusted. That's precisely what I was doing. I wouldn't even try to sing. I was just tossing my arms in the air when he captured it on tape. I had a 102-degree fever and was dying at the end of the day. I exited the warehouse where we were shooting and entered the bathroom that served as a changing room. The guy with the camera followed me the entire time. When I got to the door, I spun around and gave the cameraman a foul look before slamming the door in his face and writing MEN on it. That's how the video concludes.

What a fantastic director, Mark Fenske. It was the most successful video of our careers, one of the most successful MTV videos of all time, and Crystal Pepsi paid us $2 million to use it in a soda pop commercial. I can't believe all those people had to beat me up so badly before I folded in, but the treatment was truly atrocious. The video was fantastic. Betsy, on the other hand, was back home, overjoyed. She was getting stronger. They placed her on medicines, and she snapped out of it and began doing really well. She'd dropped a lot of weight—Betsy wasn't obese, but she, like any woman who'd had a couple of kids, had struggled with her weight. The medications made her thin. I was prepared to begin taking them. Every day, I ran on the beach or rode my bike into Santa Monica and back. She was surrounded by roses and horses. Betsy was the Beatrix Potter type. She began taking tennis lessons. I should have been happy, but instead I was thinking to myself, "I am damn near over this."

She had exhausted me. That marriage was over for me. I wasn't going to abandon her; I was going to make sure she was okay, but I was done with it. She'd exhausted me in a year. I had to hug her and rock her to sleep every night. I needed to feed her. I had to make certain that she ate. It was like having an ailing child to me. She was doing wonderful when she was on her medication, riding her horses, playing tennis, walking on the beach, and just being a normal person, as she hadn't been since I met her. I was happy for her, but she had been squeezing me for so long.

She had forgotten who she was. During that year, she was completely broken down, in and out of mental facilities. She had forgotten who she was. When she started taking Prozac and awoke from her trance, she was this joyful person living in this magnificent Malibu house with nice cars, horses, and money to burn. She had no recollection of anything. She developed a shopping addiction. She had items in her wardrobe, expensive designer sweaters and gowns that she would never wear in a million years and that she had just purchased and stored. That year, she spent close to a million dollars on her credit card. It didn't even occur to me. Betsy wanted me to exit the business after she'd calmed down, especially since my other enterprises were doing well. She wanted something to take her mind off things. I advised her to contact a realtor and look at properties. She had a budget of $2 million. I knew it would keep her occupied.

She eventually purchased a home in Carmel by the Sea. All Betsy had ever wanted was to live in Big Sur. We were at the Highlands Inn in Carmel about ten years ago, and I was jogging through the area. I dashed past the most amazing house I'd ever seen. It was a Frank Lloyd Wright-style house that appeared like an upside-down boat, sitting on the cliff, with waves splashing into the windows. It featured a massive copper roof with a big spine on top, like a boat's keel. I took Betsy to see it, but she didn't see it because there was a storybook castle across the street. It was for the best. I'd never dug it there—it was too vast, spacey, weighty, and lonely for me. We'd go down there every now and then and spend a week hiking and relaxing on the beach, but it never felt like a place I could call home.

Anyway, ten years later, Betsy was looking for a house when she called to tell she had found one. We drove down to the house I had tried to show her ten years ago. We acquired it and Betsy threw a fortune into it, completely redoing it.

Unfortunately, it had little effect. Sure, she was busy, but our relationship was as strained as ever. Our relationship was over, but I couldn't leave her because of our history. I'd been in this situation before and wanted to abandon Betsy several times—not out of cruelty, but out of necessity. It was as though she was saying, "I can't live like this anymore." Many people go through this and remain together. They simply learn to live separately for the rest of their lives, whether in separate bedrooms or elsewhere. We weren't sleeping in separate bedrooms because we were still sexually active. But all that remained of our relationship was sex, our children, and an empire. We had homes, businesses, and automobiles. Divorce was an unpleasant concept. I would never have gone through it if I had understood how bad it was. But it wasn't only the agony of divorce; I really didn't want to leave her. I still had feelings for her.

I'm the type of person that can put my head in the sand as well as put my head in the clouds as well as anyone else. I'm pretty upbeat about whatever I do in life. When I go into something, I don't believe there is any disadvantage. Believe me, I've been let down a few times, but it hasn't destroyed my optimism. I assumed things would only get better. It didn't matter because I was so preoccupied with my thoughts all the time.

I decided I was willing to stick it out once I knew she was okay and could be alone. I'd go on tour as much as I could, fucking about and getting out of the house whenever feasible. I envisioned her improving, but not our relationship. I didn't think that was ever going to happen again. It wasn't even on the top of my priority list. I was exhausted from caring for her for a year. I wasn't going to put in more effort or try to make this relationship work as I had a year before when I told the men I wasn't going on tour. That was something I was never going to do again. I was hopeful that she would improve, but in the meantime, I was going to do my thing. I accepted that this was going to be a disaster.

I went on the For Unlawful Carnal Knowledge Tour and started messing about. I wasn't fully free, and I was extremely careful not to get caught, and very careful not to bring home any virus. I wasn't careless. I was quite cautious. I was concerned about my wife. It's not like I didn't care about her. We had simply grown apart. Everything else remained the same. I still cared about her family. I still cared for our family. I even enjoyed our way of life. She couldn't bear my job, which I enjoyed. She was madly in love with horses, and I couldn't care less. We'd become completely different people.

I was partying like I'd never party before until I got out on that tour. I had always been a conservative partygoer, but as Betsy got better, everything changed. I'd phone home at night after she'd taken her Prozac. I'd say I was going out to dinner and wouldn't be able to call later. "Okay," she'd say, "then call me in the morning." Free admission. On that tour, I started having as much fun as a rock star could. I had all the money in the world, as well as all the beauties a guy could desire. I was having a great time. I was the lead singer in the world's biggest rock band, and I took full use of the opportunity. I was eating in the best restaurants, drinking the best wine, flying on private jets, and walking onstage in front of sold-out crowds. The only thing lacking was...Nothing seemed to be missing.

I screwed everyone who walked by. Under the stage, I had my own tiny tent. Eddie had brought his tent. Mike and Al both had one. We each had our own tiny tent. Mike and Al were on the other side of the fence. Eddie and I were on the same side because Eddie, like me, was a dirty dog. I dispatched roadies into the crowd to bring back the girls I had identified. During Eddie's twenty-minute guitar solo, I'd have five or six naked girls in my tent, all of us having brutal sex while Eddie was out there doing his thing. I had to stuff my hard-on back into those tight pants when I went back out. I'd put on my robe for the next few songs. That was the case every night.

That way, I'd be able to separate the good ones. We'd keep going after the show. I'd had so much sex that I couldn't come back. I'd leave for two or three weeks without returning. It seemed as though I were empty. I could fuck five different girls all night. Some of the finest sex I've ever had. This was a big hit with John Kalodner. He'd accompany us on the journey and line them up in his room. I'd be like a machine going up there. "I've just never seen anything like this," he explained. Kari then entered the picture. In October 1991, I saw her at the conclusion of the For Unlawful Carnal Knowledge Tour. Every night, I had a different woman. Scotty Ross, our tour manager, was celebrating his birthday in Richmond, Virginia. Scotty was a big fan of Leffler, so he threw him a party in his hotel suite.

Kari and two of her pals attended the party. Her boyfriend, Buffalo Bills quarterback Jim Kelly, knew the concert promoter, so they were welcomed. I was attempting to approach one of her pals since she appeared to be more available. Kari appeared to be a fun girl, incredibly cool and attractive, but I was pursuing pussy.

Betsy was at home, taking medication. She was renovating her ideal home in Carmel, right on the cliffs of Big Sur. I didn't want to go home at all.

When Kari stated she had to leave to judge a beauty pageant at some nightclub, Eddie and I agreed to accompany her. We returned later for Ed Leffler's celebration. When something we were eating fell on the floor, I was good and hammered, still attempting to pick up on Kari's girlfriend. When I looked down, I noticed Kari's feet. They're like fingers—really bony and exquisite, the longest, most beautiful toes I'd ever seen.

I raised my head again. I just couldn't stop myself. "You have really beautiful feet," I said.

I noticed how lovely she was as I looked up and saw her face and eyes. "You like those cheetos?" asked her girlfriend.

She referred to her toes as "cheetos." "Yes, I do," I replied. "I'd eat them fuckers right now."

I started hitting on Kari. Everything was in order. We were having a great time simply conversing. I asked her to my room at the conclusion of the evening, at two o'clock in the morning.

"Oh, no," she exclaimed. "We'll accompany you to your room. You've been ruined. You should get some rest. You have a performance tomorrow."

She and her two buddies escorted me to my room. When I opened the door, she offered me a small hug. "Damn," I thought, "I've wasted all this time and now I'm going to bed by myself?" I asked her if she wanted to see the show the following night.

"I can't," she said. "I've got to take my grandmother to a wedding."

Van Halen's lead vocalist, who is headlining the Richmond Coliseum, invites her to the event, and she declines? She's going to a wedding with her grandmother? It appealed to me. She had me right there and then.

"What time are you leaving?" she inquired. "I'll try to make it back."

I provided her with my hotel pseudonym. She called the following night. "We're hauling ass in the car," she explained. "We're going to do our best." Put our names on the list if we don't. We'll be there."

They arrived exactly in time, and Kari was dressed as a bridesmaid. They went into the other room and began pulling their clothing off. I took a glance. They weren't naked, but they were stripping down to their bra and underwear and throwing on some jeans. Kari appeared to be one of the most beautiful women I had ever seen in my life. And tonight, I believe, is the night. We were backstage at the concert. Scotty Ross pushed open the dressing room door, still buzzed from his birthday bash. "Scotty, this is Kari," I introduced myself.

"Nice to meet you," he remarked before puking on the floor. I was dressed like a rock star, and this man walked in and blew it all over my dressing room floor.

She wasn't bothered by it. I tried to kiss her on the way back from the show in the back of the limo. She kissed me on the cheek. I had my arm over her and stared down at her knees for a moment. Kari has long, lovely legs, as well as slender fingers, arms, and toes. She's a thin, lovely woman with flawless skin. Her knuckles appeared to be made of porcelain. I knelt and kissed her knee.

I made her have goosebumps. I saw them after she got them. "That was really sweet," she said.

I requested her to return to my room once more. "No, I can't stay over," she explained, "but I'd love to see you again."

Whoa. Isn't tonight the night? I put her in a massive lip-lock. We swapped phone numbers, and I left town the next day with the band. I called her four days later. "Will you come see me on my birthday if I send you a plane?" I said.

"Are you kidding me?" she exclaimed. "Of course, I would." She needs to give me some pussy right now. She doesn't have anywhere to go. I dispatched a jet to take her up. It was a last-minute arrangement. I was already on stage by the time she arrived for the gig. My fucking heart just started flipping and fluttering when I spotted her on the side of the stage. Pow. I fucked up and fell in love. I saw her and thought, Shazam, there she is, my dream woman.

I'm fucking anything and everything four or five times a night when I bite the bait. I gulped it down. I'm still in the boat, fumbling around. I exited the stage when Eddie was performing his solo, and instead of four or five girls waiting for me, I'm sitting there holding hands with Kari like a schoolboy.

After the show, in the dressing room, the promoter and Leffler had a huge cake for my birthday, and a naked stripper emerged from it. Not just any stripper, but the ugliest, fattest, cellulite-ridden woman they could locate. There's no way to explain how a girl like her could do this for a living. I sat there, staring at Kari, trying to be this high-class person, and thinking I was screwing it up. But she laughed. I said to myself, "I love this girl."

I informed her that she would not be returning home, and she agreed to stay for a few days. My Red Rocker tandem bicycle was shipped to me. I couldn't leave her alone. When she returned, I tried to go a week without her to put myself to the test. I never fucked another girl after that. I did not receive a blow job. I did nothing since all I cared about was her. It was too much for me. And, after nearly four months apart, we were set to return home for the holidays. That was extremely difficult. She arrived and drove for another week. I was bruised. I didn't want to return home. That was the end of it after she spent a week with me. I was finished. I was madly in love. I was going to go home and try it again with my wife. I returned home two weeks before Christmas in 1991. Betsy had finished repairing the house in Carmel. I stayed for three or four days before waking up in the middle of the night and telling Betsy that I had to leave. She was taking medicine. Betsy, the most jealous lady in the world, told me it was fine to do whatever I wanted. This was the point at which I wrote "Amnesty Is Granted."

I believed I could finally leave Betsy since she was on so much medication that she could finally deal with it. I was never certain before. One of the reasons I never left her before was because I was afraid she was suicide. I didn't want her to kill herself because of me. That was too much for me to bear. Betsy is unlike any other woman. She is not totally at home in this world. She is harmless, vulnerable, and sensitive, but she struggles to function. She is allergic to pesticides. She is unable to consume some meals. She is incredibly clever and talented, but she is not physically powerful. I finally approached Betsy one night in Carmel. I had a nervous breakdown. I burst into tears. I told her I was going to Mill Valley to clear my thoughts and figure out some issues. She was so high on tranquillisers and mood enhancers that she dismissed it as unimportant.

"It's all right, honey. You simply require some time. Come back whenever you're ready. If you have a girlfriend and want to move back in with her, I'm fine with that. I'm not concerned about what you've done. It's fine."

I didn't tell her I had a girlfriend, that I'd fallen in love, that I'd been seeing 75 females a week and suddenly fell in love. I had no idea how to deal with it. I hadn't felt this deeply in love in a long time. I jumped in my car and drove back to Mill Valley. I called Kari and asked her to come visit me. "I've just left my wife," I explained.

"Oh, my God, that's terrible," she cried, "but I'm with my grandmother, my mother, and my father." We're beginning our Christmas tradition. "I'm not sure I can do it."

I eventually got her to agree, and I sent her an airline ticket. I met her at the airport and drove her up to Mill Valley. I was really uneasy. It was just before Christmas, and leaving Andrew, five, broke my heart. Betsy then phoned. She had determined that we should spend Christmas together.

"We've got a Christmas tree in the back of the truck," she revealed. "Andrew and I will be there. We've got a Christmas tree and a turkey on the way to Mill Valley."

Betsy had this truck I built for her out of an old '53 Chevy pickup and a brand-new Chevy drive train. Betsy, the horse girl, was smitten with the truck. She had a two-hour drive. She had not comprehended a single thing I had said about leaving her.

I was unable to meet Betsy and Andrew when they arrived. Kari and I got in the car and drove to the airport. First, we returned to see her parents, where she apologised to her grandparents for missing Christmas. "If I'm going to do this, you're going to meet my parents," she explained. "You're going to look my grandmother in the eyes and say, 'I'd like your girl to accompany me.'" I sincerely apologise. This is the first Christmas she will not spend with you.'"

We went back to Virginia, where I met her folks. Her stepfather was enraged ("That son of a bitch," he said from the other room, "who does he think he is?"). We eventually became best friends, but he didn't appreciate me fleeing with his kid. We flew to the Virgin Islands and stayed at La Samanna, a French resort. I was hiding somewhere. Only Leffler was aware of my whereabouts. We had fallen in love. We were there for a month. Every several days, I called Betsy. She had no idea I was gone for good. She'd advise me to take my time and return when I was ready. Betsy never recovered, as far as I could tell. She's a wonderful mother and a highly brilliant and caring person. But I had a feeling there was a screw loose that wouldn't tighten back up.

When I finally told her brother, Bucky, about it, his first comments were, "I don't know how you did it that long."

CHAPTER 7

RIGHT HERE, RIGHT NOW

The For Unlawful Carnal Knowledge Tour had been our most successful to date. We sold out so quickly. We were performing two and three nights in the amphitheatres, a developing end of the rock concert field in the 1980s, these gigantic holes dug out of suburban dirt that housed twice as many people as the indoor arenas (often referred to as "sheds" in the business). We'd agreed to perform the live album, Right Here, Right Now, at the end of the For Unlawful Carnal Knowledge Tour, if only to get a record out quickly. As the trip came to an end, we recorded and filmed Right Here, Right Now in Fresno. Kari and I had set out on a rocket ship after that Christmas with her. We flew to Maui and stayed for three months, and the Van Halen brothers were supposed to be in the studio mixing the live record while Kari and I were out on our rocket ship. It should have been straightforward, but because the brothers were bored in the studio, they decided to take the live album.

That's when we started stumbling into each other. I can see what happened now that I look back. Al's marriage had failed. Eddie's marriage has been on the rocks for quite some time, according to Valerie. Eddie was completely intoxicated for the majority of the period. Eddie visited Betty Ford Clinic. He went to rehab a couple times. It was seldom longer than a handful of weeks. Nobody changed when Al stopped drinking. Eddie was drinking in his presence. But when Eddie got out of rehab, the studio suddenly became a no-booze zone, despite the fact that I never hung around drinking beers. After we finished recording, I'd bring in a bottle of tequila, and Mike and I would take a few shots, laugh, and have a nice time. Of course, Ed would do them as well. He wasn't drunk. He'd keep everything at the studio, while Valerie stayed in the house next door.

He had no desire for me to return home. "Why do you have to go home right now?" he'd ask. "Wait a second, I have one more thing." That bit bothers me. We'll have to recut that. You need to re-sing this item." He didn't want to go home, so he wanted to keep me as late as he could. Because he couldn't get back out to his stockpile after he got home. And Valerie knew I was gone as my car left their driveway and she saw the lights and heard the engine and the gate open and close. Because he wasn't on top of things, he was getting all messed up late at night and making foolish statements. There was always an explanation. He'd never admit to wanting me to stay because he didn't want to go home. Valerie is at home, and he is in the studio. Valerie departs, and he remains in the house, drinking.

Our disagreements intensified as the problem grew larger. Eddie Van Halen, the humble kid under his big brother's thumb, wanted to take over his band. He'd always been passive-aggressive, but it was becoming tough to cope with. He'd seem humble and back down from conflicts, but then he'd go behind my back and complain to Leffler about how hard I wasn't working. That is exactly what occurred when Kari and I went to Hawaii. The Van Halen brothers began to panic out, berating me for not being present to rehearse the new studio sessions with them. I'd abandoned my wife, and now I didn't want to go to rehearsal. Screw that.

The issue was that they'd re-recorded nearly the entire live CD. They're adjusting things because Eddie was out of tune or Al had sped up or slowed down. Everything was fixed. My singing is off-key just now that Eddie is playing in tune. And, unlike Al in "Runaround," I'm suddenly singing ahead of the beat. I had to return to the studio and redo all of my vocals. I wanted to murder those people.

Kari and I returned to Los Angeles by plane from Hawaii. I told Eddie to get out of there as soon as possible. They put me in a room with a DVD of the show, handed me a microphone, and I stood there singing the entire fucking concert once. It was exactly like a live performance. I scarcely returned to repair anything. I finished in three hours and then went out to dinner. The brothers were enraged. They took out the microscope and examined for areas that were not reasonable and needed to be repaired again. I went out to fix something when they noticed it. You're a scumbag.

Betsy had filed for divorce while Kari and I were cruising around the world. I hadn't returned home since the holidays. It broke my heart to leave Andrew, who was five years old, behind, and I wouldn't see him for years. The divorce would be contentious. It would be difficult and costly. Betsy hired a lawyer who was looking over everything. He wanted to hire a recording engineer to go over all the unrecorded music and song ideas on cassettes I had at home in case I wrote any songs in the future based on material I started while we were still married. I tried to prevent everything from happening by making a settlement offer that would have given her more money than she earned three years and millions of dollars in attorney fees later. Leffler created a way for me to pay the entire amount in one stroke. He informed me that Geffen would pay a lot of money for a greatest-hits album—something I'd never done before—and that if I wrote a few new songs, I'd get substantial publishing advances for each of them. He calculated that a single CD containing the two new songs would cover the whole expense of the divorce.

When I went to visit my attorney, who had created the agreement, Eddie and Al were sitting next to each other in his office, as they do when they're nervous. They wouldn't let me do the album. I told them I was going to do it and that it would cover my divorce expenses. They fought and fought some more. They argued it would be bad for the band. They'd never said anything to me before. They were very much behind-the-scenes people. They had a few conversations, worked each other up, began freaking out, and began seeking ways to block me from doing something I wanted to do. Eddie knew very little about his employer. He had no notion where his money was, probably. After hearing about it from my lawyer, Eddie was intrigued about how he could land a publishing agreement. I informed him that he already had a contract for publication. They simply did not want me to do something that was out of their hands. It wasn't long before they started talking to their own lawyers about suing me or kicking me out of the band.

Warner Bros. raised the price because this was supposed to be a double-record album. This hurt sales. It peaked at number five on the charts, making it our first album not to top the charts. In the summer of 1993, we started on another enormous tour to promote the live album, and we made a lot of money. Even if the tour was big, the Van Halen brothers convinced me that I wasn't doing enough. "Imagine how much money we'd make if you could sing five nights a week." They weren't bothered by my voice. "If you can't sing, just dance," they'd say.

We began to argue more frequently, and things grew less friendly. I eventually learned to fly on my own. I'd travel back home by myself. I'd stay in a few different hotels. At the end of the tour, Eddie and I weren't getting along. The fact that Ed Leffler became ill in the middle of the trip made matters worse. At the start of the journey, he detected a lump in his throat, which turned out to be cancer. He quickly had it removed and was back on the road. He even stopped smoking for a period, albeit this did not last. But it was obvious that he wasn't doing well. He was always sweating, pale, and losing weight. The cancer reappeared. He treated it with chemotherapy and radiation, but it spread. He had completed his task. Only a few weeks had passed. He went from being a person on tour with us who got pussy, did blow, drank, and had a fantastic time to being in his mid-fifties and now dying. He was tired and sick, but he stuck with us on the drive.

We played at an amphitheatre in Costa Mesa, California, for the final two nights of our tour in August 1993. I was feeling down about Leffler, so I changed my regular acoustic piece, "Eagles Fly," to "Amnesty." Since we were back in town, all of Eddie's bad-news buddies turned up with drugs and prostitutes, and he was completely wasted. He chose to change the tubes in his amplifier in the middle of my song. I'm out there performing this song, and Eddie is panicking and lowering his equipment behind me. I'm trying to make this sensitive tune, and it's driving me insane. I'm performing "Amnesty Is Granted" on acoustic, and Eddie is testing his tone to see whether the tubes are working, messed up out of his mind.

I leapt off the stage and grabbed him. We got into it, but Leffler separated us. I returned for the encore, hoping to see Eddie. I was about to kick his a$$ right here and right now. Leffler threw me in the back of a car and drove away. Later, I received a call from Al informing me that not only had we not performed an encore for the first time, but Ed Leffler had fallen. His legs became numb on him, causing him to collapse and be unable to stand. They had him on the ground.

Eddie apologised, and I returned the next night. That was his personality. He'd do the most heinous things you could imagine, and then the next day he'd be modest and pathetic, crying and holding you. It was simple to forgive this guy since his humility reached all the way to the bottom. The next day? He's a completely different person.

The following night, our final gig of the tour and our second night in Costa Mesa, we put on one of the best shows we'd ever put on. We were exhausted and exhausted. The tour had come to a close. For the first time in a long time, we went out there and played from a completely different location. We put up a very emotional performance. Every song sounded as if everyone meant it. We weren't just putting on a show. We set fire to our encores and everything else. Ed Leffler was admitted to the hospital the next day.

We went through all of this nonsense to save Leffler's life. I found a lady who sent urine samples to Mexico, where they extracted the neurotransmitters and returned them in small vials. You inject it into your muscle every day, not intravenously. Ed was forced to do it. It was something I did with him. Then there was the purple slime that turned your skin violet. We put his feet in it, ostensibly to absorb all the toxins. We attempted everything. He was wandering about, inhaling from a tank of oxygen. With all of these different treatments, we kept him alive for about a month. He had given up hope. Leffler would simply look you in the eyes and say, "Sure, okay, I'll try it." He was a very intelligent man, but he didn't believe in hocus-pocus. By October, I was planning a birthday trip to Mexico with Michael Anthony. I had gone to see Leffler the day before in the hospital. He was in poor health. They were extracting a litre of fluid from his lungs every day. He was high on morphine. He requested that I rub his hands. He was unable to feel anything. I'm giving Leffler a hand massage. I ask who we should hire to manage the band. "Just stay away from Howard Kaufman," he suggested.

It was impossible for me to believe. Howard Kaufman managed Heart, the Seattle rock band including the two Wilson sisters, and Leffler had a grudge from when Kaufman had kicked Heart and all the other bands he managed out of my travel firm because he assumed Leffler owned it. Leffler didn't care who ran us when he died, but he buried his enemies. A few days later, Eddie and Al called me in Mexico and told me that if I wanted to see Leffler alive again, I needed to return immediately. I didn't want to leave because I had a large birthday party planned. I called the hospital and spoke with Leffler, who assured me that everything was alright and that I should remain where I was. I was on my way to the cantina with my brother the next night when I felt a cold wind sweep through me. I turned to face my brother.

"Wow, I just got the loneliest feeling—I'm lonelier than I've ever felt in my life," I exclaimed.

I had no idea Leffler had died. I hadn't even considered Ed Leffler. To be honest, I was thinking about the job. Something walked straight through me as I walked out into this gorgeous, warm Cabo night. I felt as though I was the only person on the earth.

I received the call at the club. Leffler had passed away. Just like my father. My brother was present and witnessed the event. I finished the show and boarded a plane the next morning. I attended the funeral and gave a little statement in memory of Leffler. When he died, they buried him with a gram of blow and a bottle of J&B Scotch. His friends were a cast of characters. They didn't take it lightly or unkindly, but they did insane things. Ed Leffler's career was over.

CHAPTER 8

CABO WABO

In December 1983, I spotted a photograph in People magazine from Keith Richards and Patti Hansen's wedding. They were standing poolside at the Twin Dolphin, Mexico's only real hotel at the time, and I thought they looked cool. He's always been one of my heroes, and I told Betsy we should go down and look around. There was just one flight each week—one in and one out—and two locations to stay, with muddy roads leading from the airport to the Twin Dolphin. There were no phones, newspapers, televisions, or air conditioning. You had to go downtown to the phone company and pay by the minute once they placed the call for you. Keith had meant to stay for a week when he came down for his wedding, but he didn't leave for three months. His family returned home after a few weeks, but he stayed, sleeping on people's floors. Jorge Viaa, the Twin Dolphin's bellman who later became the Cabo Wabo's manager, drove Keith everywhere. Keith enjoyed performing with mariachi bands. They had no idea who he was, this crazy gringo dressed in rock-and-roll garb, but he was sipping tequila straight from the bottle and handing out $100 notes, so they liked him.

Keith stole Jorge's car and drove into town, about seven miles from the Twin Dolphin, to make a phone call. He never returned. Nobody had a car down there, so Jorge persuaded the manager to drive him downtown after midnight to search for Keith and his car. He noticed his automobile parked in the long-closed service station. Keith was passed out on the floor next to the service station worker, with a couple of empty tequila bottles beside him, when he looked inside. He most likely stopped to grab some gas and possibly directions.

I fell in love with Betsy and went down there quickly after hearing about Keith's wedding. It was a stunningly gorgeous location. You'd be walking on the beach when a wave crashed on the coast, launching a five-pound red snapper into the sand. You only had to reach down and take it up. Snorkelling anywhere in the rocks would yield oysters. You could almost capture a fish with your hands. There was no one within miles. During the summer, the place was mostly closed, and if you didn't want to eat the terrible meals at one of the hotels, your best chance was a neighbourhood taco stand or someone's house. Latinos are generally welcoming of strangers, even folks they encounter on the street, to eat at their homes. In Cabo, I used to eat at people's houses all the time. While I was out there, I came upon Guadalajara, a little palapa shanty outside of town with no windows or doors. There were chickens racing around. I sat down and asked, "What do you have?" in my little fake Spanish—Betsy spoke Spanish very well, but I was lost—"What do you have?"

"Pollo, frijoles, arroz, cerveza, chips, and salsa," said the man. Outside, across the street from the marina, he noticed two children, little more than eight years old, holding a large swordfish on a pole with a hole bored through its eyeballs. Each child had one end of the rod and was dragging the enormous fish. The individual turned around. "And fresh fish," he added.

He walks over to the kids, hands them money, grabs a knife, and whap, whap, slices a couple of large steaks off the darn thing. They walk down the road to the next eatery, carrying the fish their father had just caught. I requested the fish. I assumed I'd died and gone to heaven. This was the coolest thing I'd ever done in my life—sitting there with a brew in hand, no cars in sight, and chickens wandering around. The chickens devour the crumbs you put down. When you see a bird on the grill, you know where it came from.

Jorge drove me to town about the third time I went, still before I joined Van Halen in 1985. There were no paved roads. You couldn't get down there by car. You'd run out of gas in the middle of nowhere. When I initially drove there, we had to sleep on the side of the road at a petrol station while we waited for it to open. There were only a few food shacks there, but you could see the marina from a place in town. I decided to construct a bar. I'd already tried authentic tequila and fallen in love with it. I directed Jorge to locate a piece of property for me. I got a phone installed in Jorge's home so that we could communicate. They ran the wire from the phone company office to his house, wrapping it around stop signs. He was fortunate to reside downtown.

Terraso, a new development, was being built on the most magnificent length of beach in the area. When I initially saw it, they only had one condo completed, but I bought it right away and moved there for the summer. Cabo was deserted at that time of year. Everything was shut. Half the time, you couldn't even find a restaurant open. All of the condo units were vacant. I had a couple of acres on the beach to myself, as well as a massive swimming pool.

I have started going down every October because my brother's birthday is on October 8, my sister's is on October 11, and my birthday is on October 13. I went my mother, my brothers and sisters, and their families to the Twin Dolphin for two weeks to celebrate our birthdays. Bucky shipped down one of my hot-rod mountain bikes, and I spent every day riding the dirt roads around Cabo. Jorge informed me of a triathlon organised by the local military post but open to the public one year. I registered. Because the city offered a $1,000 cash prize, the race drew a lot of attention. The entire town gathered at the marina to watch as about 150 contestants swarmed the wharf where they would swim the first lap, a quarter-mile across the water. I was wearing a standard banana hammock and Speedos, but everyone else simply stripped to their underwear and hopped in. I resisted. Many of these people had no idea how to swim and were splashing and struggling.

I dove in and began swimming across. When I got out, a small, stocky guy took off down the beach, leaving me in the dust, although I was among the top four or five guys. We arrived at the third leg, the cycling section, and Jorge was there for me, holding my bike. Only about half of the racers still racing down the beach behind us had bikes. I had no idea what the others would do. They did have bikes, but they were destroyed, large, hefty clunkers with missing tires, whereas I had this lightweight, ten-speed mountain bike. They'd never seen anything like it before down there. I was starting to feel like the biggest jerk on the planet. The short, stocky guy was riding his junky piece of steel ahead of me. He was dying up the hill when I flew by him in my mid-gears.

I was so far ahead of him that I was barely breathing when he crossed the finish line. I looked at Jorge and handed him the award and the cash. He grabbed both of them, turned around, and lifted his hands above his head as if he had won the race. He never even thanked me. That made Jorge and me giggle for days. The more time I spent down there, the better it got, and once I joined Van Halen, Cabo became a crucial part of my songwriting process. I used to jam new songs with Ed, Al, and Mike and make up lyrics while I scattered along. Then I'd travel to Cabo. I'd go to the beach, finish my lyrics, and then come back to do my vocals. A number of songs from OU812 were inspired by my writing down there. "Sucker in a 3 Piece" originated in Cabo. I saw this stunning girl poolside at the Twin Dolphin who was married to this old dude, and this female was giving me signals despite the fact that I was married and she was with this affluent guy, the "Sucker in a 3 Piece."

One Sunday about 9:30 a.m., I was driving down a rural road with a barbed-wire fence to my favourite taco restaurant for breakfast. In front of me, a man was staggering along the road. I couldn't get past him. He bounced off the fence into the road ahead of me, then back into the barbed wire. He was bleeding down his leg and lacked a shoe. He was a local who'd been drinking mescal all night. I was watching him drive down the road like that when I realised he was doing the Cabo Wabo. I returned to my pad and began writing the lyrics. "Been to Rome, Dallas, Texas, man, I thought I'd seen it all— round the world, around every corner, man, I thought I'd hit the wall." "Cabo Wabo," the entire song, poured out of me. Because I had one of the only phones in Cabo, I dialled Eddie's number and said, "Eddie, listen to this." In my imagination, I penned the song to the music of "Make It Last," one of the first songs I wrote in Montrose. I sang it over the phone to him.

"Oh, man, listen to this," he remarked. "Last night, Al and I worked on this." He played some music that sounded similar to "Make It Last."

It worked over the phone. I flew back to Los Angeles early so I could perform the song. While I was away, they recorded the music. I entered. I brought a handheld microphone with me. I was going to scat, but I read the lyrics off my notepad from start to finish, and that song was finished. My vocals on OU812 sound odd because of that crappy little handheld mike, but it was such a wonderful vocal take that we unanimously chose to preserve it. Jorge finally discovered a piece of property for the bar I'd planned to build after nearly four years of searching, but it was going to be pricey. Even though I was in Van Halen, I didn't have enough money for a million-dollar project; rather, I had enough money for a half-million-dollar endeavour. However, that was a lot of money to invest in a village with dirt roads and no telephones.

However, the town has been gradually growing. They hadn't paved any of the side streets, but they had paved the road to town and part of the way through town. The Hollywood swinging set began to explore the town. The hipsters were on their way down. It was no longer just a small fishing village. Boat owners and private-plane pilots discovered the location. This dirt strip would be used for private plane landings. Walking around, you could feel the potential, but it wasn't quite there.

I knew I was going to call Cabo Wabo's cantina. The song was already written. It was supposed to be a tequila bar with a stage. I urged Jorge to locate an architect, and he identified Marco Monroy Jr., the son of Terrasol's developer, whom I had met. When I was exploring venues, his father had shown me a smelly, old sardine factory. His kid had just graduated from college and was starting to work for his father. He had constructed a couple of the coolest houses down there. He was hired by me.

Marco devised the strategy. It looked amazing. I assumed the structure was three thousand square feet, but Marco and Jorge were speaking in metres. I assumed there would be plenty of space for a large parking lot. The foundation was three times larger than I anticipated when they laid it. I was envisioning a lovely, little area that could hold 50 or 60 people, at most 150. With everything going on, Eddie and Al couldn't help but notice that my ideas for my cantina were getting a lot of my attention. Finally, Ed Leffler told me that the other Van Halen members were starting to feel left out. He'd approached me and gently recommended that I make the other gentlemen my cantina companions.

"You want MTV to really support it, the press, the publicity," he'd stated. "Bring these guys in on it."

We had a meeting, and everyone, including Leffler, decided to work together as equal partners. They each handed me $70,000 to make up for the money I'd put up. It was successful. In April 1990, Van Halen performed at the gala grand opening weekend. MTV invested millions of dollars on a large promotional campaign. They made ads and organised competitions. They flew an entire planeload of folks down there. Raquel Welch was in attendance. Boston's Brad Delp and Toto's Steve Lukather. The entire community was ecstatic.

Betsy's plane panic had happened a year previously, and she hadn't flown since. She was starting to come around by the big opening of the cantina, and the medication was starting to work, but she refused to board an aircraft. My plane was still there, but I couldn't fly down there without her. I purchased a motor home to transport everyone to the grand opening. I invited my brother-in-law and sister, as well as Betsy, the babysitter, and the kids, to accompany me. Driving down took three days. It was my second time driving down, and it was difficult. I wanted to kill Betsy by the time I arrived. I dispatched my plane down to Cabo with her psychiatrist, our doctor, their families, and a couple of my friends in the middle of the drive. I loaded eight people onto that thing and flew them down in my plane while driving a fucking 32-foot mobile home for three days.

Betsy adored Cabo but was terrified of everything. She was terrified that she might have another panic attack. She hadn't returned since the previous time she flipped out. She was apprehensive about returning to the same Terrasol condo. She was in very horrible shape. We were on the outskirts of town, about twenty minutes from the property, showing our friends one of her favourite beaches, when she became agitated. They should go for a walk on the beach, according to the psychiatrist.

He was attempting to calm her down because she was shaking. We sat about while they walked down the beach, attempting to give them some room. I exploded. I burst out laughing. The excitement of the big opening and the arrival of the Van Halen guys for the first time. They were all shocked as well—what, no phones in the room? What do you mean, there is no room service? I stormed over to where Betsy and her therapist were conversing.

"Fuck this," I said to the therapist. "I've got a lot of work to do." "We're leaving right now." She did, in fact, snap out of it. It jolted her awake. I knew I couldn't be too heavy with her when we got back to the condo.

We went outside to complete the sound check. Betsy's doctor arrived. He'd never seen me play before. He was simply a psychiatrist who had met Eddie. The sound check astounded the doctor. "I've never seen anything like that before in my life," he remarked.

The grand opening weekend was a success. Van Halen performed two nights. We had MTV and Mexican television. It was a huge deal that went south almost immediately.

Everything went swimmingly the first week. Nobody came to the cantina after we left and the town had emptied out. Cabo Wabo was not visited by the locals. We only had a small restaurant with a large taco bar. We handed out beverages. There wasn't much to do there. We lacked a live band. We played music through the speakers. The echo chamber measured fourteen thousand square feet. It was really dark. We had many low lights and everything was dark. It didn't have much charm yet. We built and opened this establishment. Marco was not present. Jorge, who had never done anything like this before, was in charge of the company. A plane would land once a week, and there would be people in town. The place would do well once or twice a week, but not very well. It was empty for the rest of the week.

When we first began, t-shirts were selling nicely. We were never able to persuade Jorge to send the T-shirt money. Jorge came to a halt since he lacked the funds to purchase more T-shirts. He didn't have enough money to buy more alcohol, food, or pay the employees. The place was on its last legs. It was losing roughly $10,000 per month, which is a lot of money. Jorge had no idea what he was doing.

When all of this was going on, Leffler was still alive and well. He'd flown down to settle things out and met the Deadhead son of the man who owned another hotel in another town on the plane. I recognized him from the hotel. He sat at the pub all day, drinking. Jorge was fired, and the Deadhead was put in charge. Didn't accomplish anything. He was more business-savvy, but the guy was doing drugs and drinking, and the Federales were shaking him down because they suspected he was dealing.

Van Halen only played Cabo once more, after a show in Mexico City on the cantina's second anniversary in 1992, but Mikey and I used to bring David Lauser down every year to play my birthday bash in October. Eddie and Al were dissatisfied with the location. We were asking for money every time they turned around. They each put in another $10,000 a few times. That would keep the business running for about six months. It was losing more than a hundred thousand dollars per year. They indicated they weren't going to put any more money into the cantina after a few times.

Finally, Mike and I decided to go down and play whenever the cantina needed money. The facility would be crowded after two or three nights. We would charge $5 at the door. That way, we could keep it continuing. We went to the cantina five times that year and never had to pay again.

Our Deadhead boss asked if he could introduce me one night. He appeared to be high because his jaw was moving from left to right, grinding his teeth. He stood up and began delivering jokes and stories. People were hurling objects at him and cursing at him. We had to drag him away.

When I urged him to open the safe at the office, he was so dazed that he couldn't work the combination. When he eventually opened the safe, the only item inside was a bag of coke. I let him go. I returned and informed Leffler. The entire band was enraged. It was a shambles.

He later cleaned up and apologised to everyone. He had a family and resided in that area. He was attempting to reassemble it. We had little option but to give Leffler some leeway, but the whole situation had made all of us—especially the Van Halen brothers—anxious about Cabo and where it was leading. They refused to put any more money into it and appeared to be done with the whole concept of the place. I thought we could keep on, but I realised it needed assistance. What I didn't realise was that things would only become worse when Leffler died.

CHAPTER 9

FATHER'S DAY

We auditioned managers when Leffler died. I wanted Shep Gordon and Johnny Barbis—Shep was Alice Cooper's outstanding manager, and Barbis was one of the most well-liked individuals in the industry, running labels and friends with U2, Elton John, and everyone else. The executives at Warner Bros. liked the concept. We had a meeting with them. They were disliked by the brothers. I contacted David Geffen, who recommended Elliot Roberts, Neil Young's manager. We encountered him as well, and the Van Halens blew him out in about five seconds.

Ed and Al kept me waiting for two months before telling me they wanted Ray Danniels. He was married to the sister of Al's wife and handled Rush. They said I got my man the last time, and this time they wanted their boy. Ray Danniels had been lurking in the shadows the entire time. Ray Danniels had alerted the Van Halen brothers about a publishing deal Leffler had struck on the live CD before he was even our manager. It wasn't a big problem, but Ray Danniels made the brothers believe they'd been taken advantage of. They had me repay a large quantity of money. Alex Van Halen had never written a song in his life and was earning the same amount of money from publishing as I was. Danniels acquired the brothers' trust by demonstrating that he would be on their side, not mine. At this point, Ed and Al were working against me. They assumed Leffler and I had fucked them. We didn't fuck those people. We rescued them. They made ten times as much money in one year than they had in any previous year before we joined the band. Nobody got screwed.

"They're going to sign with you," I told Ray. I'm not. You get nothing for my money." They agreed to pay management as part of the contract I negotiated. Management was not paid. He didn't do anything for me. He wasn't my boss. I'd hire my own manager. I didn't care for him. I wanted to eat his face. And he was terrified of me. He refused to enter the room with me. He kept his distance from me, always meeting with Eddie.

Ray Danniels went to Warner Bros. and had our contract renewed. He secured a few bonus points for the band's early albums—the ones I wasn't on—but nothing else changed. He renegotiated the identical deal we had before. Except for one detail. Ed Leffler had written into my contract when I joined Van Halen that after every Van Halen record, I would have the option to do a Sammy Hagar solo record for a large sum of money. I only completed one. Ed Leffler referred to it as "my golden parachute." They removed that in some way. When I entered a backstage dressing room in Toronto, Ray Danniels was there with his briefcase. Ed and Al were signing documents in front of a notary. They were signing the record agreement without even asking for my signature. "Don't worry about it," remarked Ray Danniels. "Ed and Al are all that matters in this band."

In early 1994, a few months after Leffler's death, the cokehead manager in Cabo called to tell me that he had given the keys to the employees and that the government had draped a yellow ribbon around the facility and closed it down. I couldn't think of anything else to do, so I dialled Marco Monroy's number. Marco realised that the manager had not paid any bills for the entire year. He had spent all of the money. Marco stated that the cantina owed roughly $300,000 to him. The place was a shambles. The furniture was shot, and the equipment was shattered. He wanted to be my business partner. He offered to pay off the debts and put another $100,000 into sprucing up the home.

Jorge had long since left. He got involved with an American "actress" who had some terrible habits. The issue was that everything was registered in Jorge's name. He has vanished. We had no idea where the hell he was. It was not a nice sight.

I required complete command of the cantina. The Van Halens had already urged me to stick the place up my ass, and our relationship deteriorated further when Leffler died. I approached Ray Danniels and asked if I might purchase the other partners' shares. He was attempting to gain my favour. He devised a strategy with our accountant to recoup their investment by taking a loss. They deducted it from their taxes. They returned it to me after I agreed to give them first refusal to invest if I ever built another one. They would get their investment back if I sold it within five years, albeit that would be difficult given that they had already deducted it from their taxes. I have to indemnify them for their debts and any other legal issues. It was a little complicated, but I went for it anyway.

Marco desired to have someone he knew manage the cantina. Tito was a strong guy who was married to a wealthy Mexican heiress. They lived in a home built by Marco. Tito spruced up the place. He not only tightened up the personnel, but he also got rid of the drug traffickers and lowlifes that were frequenting the establishment. Marco and I resolved to reclaim the property's title and restructure the firm. When we couldn't find Jorge, we went to see his ex-wife, who still lived in Cabo with her children. We made her a $25,000 offer. We brought an interpreter because she didn't speak English. She stood up and walked away. I'm not sure why because she ended up with nothing.

When we eventually located Jorge, he was tough as nails. He was looking for 10%. Marco and I both gave up 5% to get him to agree to everything. Soon after, he crawled back, appealing for his job. He abandoned the young lady. He had been straightened out. He returned to Cabo, and we let him in. He's been there ever since, and he's been as much a saviour of the area as Marco. The town was beginning to come together. The huge dream was coming true in Cabo. The road was now paved. There were further hotels. Three or four planes arrived each day. The town was crowded. Marco and Tito completely transformed Cabo Wabo from the start. They cleaned it up and made it seem good. We started making money within the first month.

The setting was stunning. We were putting money into it and pulling money out without any money coming out of our pockets. We made roughly $200,000 in profit our first year. The brothers were displeased. They began accusing me of running the place into the ground in order for them to give it back to me. I wish I was that intelligent. Scotty Ross, our tour manager and a bit of a jerk, returned from Cabo and marched into a Van Halen rehearsal and slapped my palm. "Cabo Wabo was jam-packed, dude," he explained. "You make a lot of money. "The place looks fantastic." The Van Halens were not happy. Mikey and I continued to visit virtually every other month. Mike was game to go along with me. He had planned to accompany me down for my birthday that year, but they wouldn't allow Mike to travel again. Mike was not permitted to travel to Cabo. They truly believed I had fucked them.

I was spending as much time as I could with Kari while Cabo was coming together. We just wanted to go do things. Every night, we stayed together. We resided in Hawaii, Mexico, and Mill Valley, California. We were going to New York. We were going to Malta. We travelled to Italy. We went wherever we wanted. We had such perfect timing. We were walking through Hana Ranch on Maui after eating some mushrooms when the notion struck us to get a parrot. We went a little further and found a cage with some parrots. This small girl approached the cage and rubbed her head against the bars, as birds do. We reached an agreement and returned her to our room. Spooch was her name. Under the covers, that bird slept with us. We were lounging in the garden by the pool as soon as we arrived home in Mill Valley. Spooch's wings were clipped so she couldn't fly away. She was perched on our shoulders. Spooch was a nanday conure, and we were discussing how we needed to get Spooch a partner when a motherfucking nanday conure flies out of the sky and settles on Spooch's cage. Spooch was conversing with the bird. The bird entered the cage to get some water. Boom. We obtained another bird. Spooky was his nickname. He never got along with Spooch— they fought all the time—and we had to give him to Bucky finally, but it happened to us.

We were in Boca Raton, Florida, not long after we met, near Kari's father's house. She desired to see her father. He acquired residences, lived in them for six months, fixed them up, moved out, and rented them out. We took a limo to supper, which was more than an hour away. We smoked a big one in the limo after dinner and got a little sexual in the backseat. Around midnight, we arrived at her father's house, and Kari took the key from the top of the water heater. We opened the door, turned on the living room light, and began rolling around on the couch. I walked on a pair of men's shoes when I put my foot on the floor. I stood up naked and turned on more lights. A shirt is draped across a chair, and an ashtray contains smoke. Someone has rented and is residing in the residence.

We raced out of there, stoned on our asses, half-naked, into the limo. Our pulses were racing. We were about to be slain, but we couldn't stop laughing. Because Kari and I were in sync, so many things happened. I was living a lie with Betsy. I was lying to her about everything, and as a result, I was lying to others on the phone since she could hear. I was this whole lie—so out of sync that nothing worked for me. I opened up to Kari as soon as I fell in love with her and never lied again. I felt liberated. I felt liberated. Everything we did was the correct course of action. Things that we desired came to us. You'd imagine it, and it'd happen. We could make each other laugh about anything. Another night, after we returned to Mill Valley, I ran into Bob Weir of the Grateful Dead at the Sweetwater, the town's modest rock club. Kari and I happened into him at a table with a girlfriend, sipping Suntory scotch straight from the bottle. We sat and drank together until the bar closed at two a.m. "Let's go to my house," he suggested. It's a good idea to have everyone come to your place and then have them drive home instead of you. "No," I replied. "Let's go over to my house."

He drove up to my house in a beat-up old Corvette that hadn't been washed in years. My driveway is quite nasty. There was no curb, just a steep drop of 250 feet. Bob arrived with a mason jar full of buds. His scotch was nearly finished. We began smoking marijuana and continued to drink. We played some guitar. We urinated on the deck.

I'm inebriated and shot around four o'clock in the morning. I told Bob that it was time for them to leave. We let them out the door, and Kari inquired if I wasn't going to assist him in getting out of the driveway. I didn't notice it. He was the Grateful Dead's Bob Weir. He was capable of looking after himself. I began climbing the stairs.

Outside, there's a dreadful loud scraping noise—Kari exclaims, "Oh, my God!"—and I run back down. Instead of backing up and turning around, he drove straight out of the driveway, and his car was now half on and half off the driveway, facing down, with the back wheels off the ground. Kari and I raced out of the house and sat on the trunk. Weir, who was sitting next to his girlfriend in the car, appeared bewildered. "I think I need to pull forward," he added.

I advised him to sit extremely still and have his girlfriend slowly climb out. She crawled out the rear and sat with us on the trunk. He followed her out the door. The car may have crashed in a split second. He's dead, no seat belt, convertible, down the hill. Bob Weir was found dead at Sammy Hagar's house. It was dreadful, and it was five o'clock in the morning. I instructed him to walk home. He wandered down the hill with his lover, carrying his mason jar of buds. I had a meeting the next morning and was quite hungover after only three hours of sleep. I backed out of the driveway, attempting to avoid hitting his car and knocking it down the hill, and broke off my goddamn $1,600 side mirror. I called a towing service. When we returned home about 5:00 p.m., the tow company had left a letter saying they couldn't take the car. They didn't have enough room behind the automobile and were concerned about pushing it over the hill. That wretched automobile took two tow trucks and three days to get out of my driveway. I even covered the cost of the tow truck. I was furious with Bob, but Kari and I just laughed.

Kari began to want to settle down a little more in the Mill Valley house after a while. She began putting her own belongings in there. She'd been sleeping in Betsy's bed and living in Betsy's house. She began to make changes. I started to notice her domestic side. She soon started talking about how she wanted to have a baby. Andrew was about ten years old. I was hesitant. But you don't say no to a woman who says she wants to have a baby. But I didn't want to be a father again. Aaron was an adult who lived in Los Angeles, but Andrew was a heartbreaker. Betsy first refused to let me see him. She eventually agreed to allow him to come up on weekends, although it was difficult for him. I'd find him crying in his room. Andrew was devastated by his divorce. That is something I will always remember. Being a father again didn't seem all that appealing. When I moved to Northern California, Miss Kellerman warned me, "Someday you're going to have two daughters." Everything else Miss Kellerman said had come true. True enough. Kari became pregnant just by bringing it up. We were in the Jacuzzi beside the pool in the middle of the day and threw it down on the grass. I was aware of it. We planned our wedding. Kari and I had been dating for over four years. Leffler had been deceased for about two years. Since that last weekend in Costa Mesa, the band has not toured. We had been working for months on a new Van Halen album, Balance, when I decided to marry in November 1995. We got married in Mill Valley at the Mount Tam Amphitheater. A lovely, beautiful day. My mother was overjoyed. Kari's grandmother, her mother, and the rest of my family were present. Emeril Lagasse, the legendary New Orleans chef, travelled in to cater the wedding. We imported ten pounds of white truffles from Italy. Ed and Al were present. Everyone posed for the People magazine photo. Someone overheard stating to the brothers, "This fucker's making way too much money."

Eddie was supposed to be sober, but he wasn't, and he was potentially dangerous. Ray Danniels was worried that we keep Eddie straight because he couldn't drink around Valerie. In 1993, I took Eddie to the Bridge School concert, an all-acoustic benefit for Neil Young's school for youngsters with severe learning difficulties. I did a few solo gigs and was terrified. I don't lack confidence at all, except when I'm alone with an acoustic guitar, in which case I'm a wreck. Neil Young is an audacious musician. He begins to stamp his foot, slap his guitar, and sing at the top of his lungs. He is devoid of inhibitions. Backstage, James Taylor was charming. "Sammy, what do you mean you're nervous?" he inquired. "We all want to be just like you."

"What do you mean," I inquired. "Scared?"

The headline act the year I brought Eddie was Simon and Garfunkel. Eddie and I were both nervous, but we performed admirably. Eddie played a solo on this tiny amp with a kind of acoustic arrangement and he was fantastic. We didn't do as well as you would have thought, but this wasn't our audience. We returned to our trailer and performed some blowing. While Eddie was getting more trashed, I started conversing with Paul Simon, who was in the trailer next to ours. He eventually went outside to check what was going on. Paul Simon asked him to play on one of his songs. "Do you know the song 'Sound of Silence'?" he said.

"No, I've never heard of it," Eddie replied.

Simon dragged him inside the trailer and attempted to show him the song. In roughly twenty minutes, he was expected to enter the stage. Eddie was unable to grasp it. I believe he was too drunk. "Wait," he advised. "What key was it again?"

He attempted finger-tapping to the music. Eddie is a fantastic musician, but he is quite systematic. He doesn't just jam those things in. He discovers and performs the melody. While Paul was singing and playing him through the song, he was looking for the melody. And he was unable to obtain it. "Never mind, Eddie," Simon explained.

"No, no, no," Eddie responded, leaning over his instrument once again. Simon finally raced to the stage and summoned Eddie, who proceeded to butcher the song.

We were making the Balance record, but Van Halen's career ended. We would not have finished that record if it hadn't been for the producer, Bruce Fairbairn. He seemed to have to kick Eddie out every night. Eddie would appear intoxicated and messed up. When you entered the studio's restroom, there would be a hole in the wall. When I reached down, there was a bag of cocaine. Under the sink was a bottle of vodka. Cigarettes and chewing gum were ubiquitous. "Al," I'd remark, "your brother messed up." What is this nonsense about his being clean and sober? "He's had his brain ripped out."

"You're crazy," Al would say. "That's just the way Ed acts."

I'd smack Eddie in the face. "Get the fuck out of here, Ed." You're messed up. I don't want you to be here with me while I'm working. I'm working on my singing. "Get the hell out of here!"

"You motherfucker, I haven't had a drink in five months," he said. He'd weep himself to sleep and smash stuff.

It got really bad. Fairbairn and I were staying at the Bel-Air Hotel, and when Eddie became really obnoxious, he would call the session and the two of us would drive back to the hotel, sit in the bar, eat a snack, and drink a couple of cocktails. Eddie was nervous because, for one thing, he required a hip replacement and was constantly on painkillers. Second, he appeared to be drinking and concealing it from everyone. Eddie began offering comments about how I should sing when I began my vocals for the first time. That gradually escalated, and Fairbairn drove me to Vancouver to do my vocals on my own. I could tell they were attempting to get rid of me. Eddie was attempting to persuade me to go. Every lyric I wrote, he'd find something wrong with it. He'd never mentioned a lyric before. He suddenly dislikes everything.

"That's wimpy," he remarked. "Make it, 'Don't tell me what love can't do.'" I had a powerful, positive thought—"I want to show you what love can do"—but Eddie had a different idea. No, I want white, not black. Okay, I'll use white. No, I prefer black. To begin with, I desired black. What do you think? I'd like white. It'd drive me insane. The brothers were dead-on-arrival.

That song, "Don't Tell Me What Love Can Do," was written about Kurt Cobain. I wanted it to say something like, "I want to show you what love can do." Ed and Al argued with me about it. They desired a more grunge, bad-attitude tune. "Don't try to tell me what love can do." That was not my intention. I was referring to someone who had the potential to save Kurt Cobain's life. That is what I believe. You have the ability to save people. People are killed by drugs. People believe that Jimi Hendrix was great because of his use of drugs. No, it was drugs that killed Jimi Hendrix. Kurt Cobain might have been rescued. For some reason, the folks around him let him go. They had to have predicted it. So I wrote that song to emphasise that you have control over your future. This is your life. You are free to do whatever you desire. But then I wanted the chorus to say, "But I want to show you what love can do." I wanted it to be a love song. Not about me or Kurt Cobain, but about what others he knew and loved could have done for him.

Kari was pregnant, and they despised my joy. I kept telling Kari that I needed to leave the band, but I didn't want to. I witnessed what they did to the other man. They will tell lies. They're going to crucify me. They're going to kill me with the fans. Roth was opposed by the crowd. As a solo artist, he died young. Perhaps not immediately—he had a brief time when he first went solo—but it wasn't long. That was something I didn't want to happen to me.

My ex-brother-in-law, Bucky, died just three weeks before the Balance Tour began in March 1995. It was heartbreaking. Bucky and Joelle had separated, and he and his son, Ben, had been living on a houseboat in Sausalito with Bucky's new lover, Penny, who used to be Jeff Beck's old lady. Bucky lived for his child, and when Ben died in a car accident—a group of kids travelling in the back of a pickup truck on their way to Stinson Beach, and Ben was the only one killed—Bucky's life was turned upside down. Bucky received a fair payout after my lawyer sued the city over the accident. When Bucky died of an overdose, they discovered the cheque crumpled in his fist.

The Van Halen brothers were in bad health by the time we went on tour that March. Because of a ruptured vertebrae, Al had to leave the tour in a neck brace. On the day of our dress rehearsal in Pensacola, Florida, Al fell in the hotel lobby. His hands went numb, and he fell. He began attending neurosurgeons on a daily basis, receiving these bizarre modifications. The doctor in Paris put on latex gloves and inserted his hand up Al's ass to work on the lower vertebrae. As if that wasn't enough, he and his wife separated, signalling the start of yet another divorce for Al. He was under a lot of strain. Eddie appeared to be on painkillers the most of the time and was facing a total hip replacement owing to avascular necrosis, a bone disease that is frequently related with drinking. Eddie had to walk with a cane since his hips were shot. He'd stroll up to the stage, set down his cane, and walk out. Because his hips were killing him, he would occasionally sit on the drum riser or a stool and perform a few tunes.

Ray Danniels hired the band to open for Bon Jovi at football stadiums in Europe during the Balance Tour's last leg in May and June 1995. It was a complete disaster. Van Halen had no business sharing a bill with Bon Jovi, who was huge in that country. They did three nights at Wembley Stadium in London, eighty thousand people per night, and when we played, there were about ten thousand people in the front going crazy, and about sixty thousand teenyboppers in the back waiting for Bon Jovi. As soon as we finished playing, our audience dispersed, and the Bon Jovi kids took their place at the front of the stage. It was completely oil and water. There's nothing against Jon Bon Jovi. On this tour, he and I ate out several times. But that was Van Halen's worst idea ever. On that tour, we got nowhere. I could feel the end approaching. Van Halen, on the other hand, rocked. We'd put on a terrific concert, walk offstage together, hugging and laughing about how great it was, and then it'd be back to the same stuff the next day.

We travelled separately to Japan to finish out the tour. We stayed in various hotels. Eddie called about two o'clock in the morning. He'd depleted his minibar. He was squandered on his ass. Sober and clean? These were almost the last performances. We were stopping in Hawaii for four nights on the way back, but that was it.

"What are you going to do when we get back?" he wondered.

It's the same old Ronnie Montrose narrative.

"I don't know," I admitted. "You should take some time off. "What are your plans?"

"I don't know yet," he admitted. "I'll let you know when I figure it out." I have some ideas, but I'll let you know whether or not they involve you."

"Okay," I replied. "Fucked you." I got off the phone.

We headed to Hawaii for the last shows. Kari and I decided to buy a house on a whim. We'd been renting homes for three months every year, from Thanksgiving through, say, January or February. I called a realtor while we were on our way to the airport. I told him I wanted something private, on the beach, with plenty of land, a guest house, a pool, and complete seclusion. I'd like to be naked. I'd like to have some fruit trees. He took us to this cliffside location on Maui. We bought the house right away and planned that after the tour, we would relocate to Hawaii to have the baby. We intended to give birth to this child naturally. I wanted to hand it over. I wanted to have the kid and step away from the band for a while.

The brothers began calling every day after the tour concluded. We'd just returned from a tour. We had just finished a record and a global tour when these insane bastards approached us about doing a song for the film Twister. It did not sit well with me. All they wanted was for me to leave the island. Ray Danniels would call and say things like, "If you're not back tomorrow, we'll assume you've quit the band."

I called the director of photography. He forwarded the script to me. Twister chasers use certain essential phrases, such as "drop down." These fantastic lyrics were written for a song named "Drop Down." I made a quick presentation over there, and the director loved it, saying I told the entire story in three minutes.

They despised it. Al and Eddie both cautioned me that writing about the movie was a bad idea. I informed them that I had been collaborating with the director.

"He doesn't know what he's talking about," they claimed. "It bothers us. Come on over here. If you aren't here tomorrow, we will assume you have left the band."

Kari was nearly due to give birth, and I was on my way home. I flew my mother over and back. I had to fly back to the mainland for the sixth time. I composed new lyrics. Bruce Fairbairn was there to greet me. Eddie had hoped to title the song "Human Beings." All these combative lyrics—"lemmings breeding...I have just enough Christ in me to feel somewhat guilty...because we are humans, human beings."

I was planning to go back to Hawaii the next day, but they asked me to remain and work on another song for the greatest-hits album. I informed them I wasn't going to do any songs for a greatest-hits album and we parted ways. I returned to my hotel room and asked the front desk to alter my name. I didn't want to phone Kari at four a.m. and tell her. Eddie had been attempting to contact me all night. Security knocked on my door to inform me that Eddie Van Halen was on the phone and wanted to know what room I was in. "What exactly do you want us to do?" the person inquired.

"Tell him to go fuck himself," I instructed.

That's when they dialled Roth's number. Ray Danniels came up with the notion for the greatest-hits collection. They were looking for a quick buck. If we're going into the studio, I thought we should produce a full album, but they wanted a greatest-hits collection. Then he has another brilliant idea: bring back David Lee Roth, record two new songs with him, and record two new songs with Sammy, and we'll be larger than God. They did everything behind my back. I was kicked out of the band for refusing to comply.

Eddie always claimed I resigned, and perhaps I did. His point of view was that I had always aspired to be a solo artist. They went so far as to criticise my work ethic. He and Alex informed MTV News' Kurt Loder that I didn't want to work. I recall Eddie saying in one story, "He was a lot older than us, and I don't think he really wanted to work like we did."

I made their Van Halen rings their trademark. They presented me with my Cabo Wabo brand. My royalties were kept by me. Because they'd already reduced Michael Anthony's share to 10%, I was a 30% partner in that band.

Things that irritate me cause me to take action. I believe I do best when I have something to prove. I was burned out and done with the business when I joined Van Halen. At that moment, I didn't even want to be creative. I sparked a fire when I replaced their first singer and was taking trash from everyone, putting myself on the spot—I'll show these motherfuckers. I got quite motivated in that band, and we accomplished some wonderful things, even at the end. Even our last album, Balance, was fantastic. I'm a sucker for adrenaline and inspiration. I will get up if something inspires me. I can accomplish anything if I am inspired. When I was fired from Van Halen, I was determined to prove to those motherfuckers that they had made the worst mistake of their lives.

CHAPTER 10

MAS TEQUILA

I was done with Van Halen. One side of me felt outraged, but the other was overjoyed.Kari and I boarded a plane with our new baby to return to Maui. We sneaked a tiny dog named Winchell on board. You cannot bring your dog to Hawaii. They keep the suckers in isolation for six months. We intended to remain for a while—I certainly didn't have any big plans—so we injected the small pooch with dog tranquillisers and packed him in a sack. Mickey Hart of the Grateful Dead sat across the aisle in the first-class compartment. I knew who he was, but we'd never actually met. He and his wife, Caryl, were on their way to the islands for some relaxation, something Mickey Hart has no idea about.

Bill Cosby was on the aeroplane as well, maybe four rows behind us. It was an early-morning flight, and we were dozing off as the jet prepared to land. Out of the corner of my eye, I hear that famous Bill Cosby voice say, "Oh, what a cute little dog."

I turned around and looked around. Winchell was staggering down the aisle, wobbling, tripping, and falling like a drunk. He was a rat terrier, and he dug his way out of his sack, unzipped it, and escaped. We were caught. Mickey's wife was a lawyer, and she sprung into action, schmoozing the stewardess. We had to remain on the plane. Bill Cosby passed me by, staring down at his suitcase and saying, "Woof...woof." Mickey and Caryl joined us. We were there for a few hours. This was a big deal. We were facing a $25,000 fine and even jail time, but after a few $100 bills were passed around, a dog carrier was brought to the plane and Winchell went into the baggage compartment to fly home with the stewardess, who handed him off to some of our friends in San Francisco who were waiting for the dog.

I had accepted that Van Halen was over when I boarded that plane to Hawaii. I was going to Hawaii since that is my sanctuary. The press would have been all over me if I had gone to Cabo. What occurred? What occurred? I just wanted to lie down and think about what to do. I was travelling to Hawaii to clear my thoughts and figure out what I really wanted. Was I sure I wanted to keep doing this? I certainly didn't have to work financially. Since Montrose, I'd been doing the tour/album, tour/album grind. I was planning to lie down and do nothing until something came to me. I had no intention of forming a band. I was planning on hiding. But Mickey Hart was having none of it. Mickey visited my Maui home every day. I told him I was done with the music industry. He told me I had to get back on the horse immediately away because I was too skilled to give up. He'd come over, fire up some huge fat joints, and have me play guitar. He had all these African music cassettes and was always putting tapes in the deck and told me, "Listen to this." That knucklehead totally got me back on the horse. Mickey is the most animated person on the planet. He's never taken a five-minute break in his life. He reads six newspapers a day, writes a couple chapters of a book, writes a couple of songs, and attends practice.

"What do you mean you're going to take some time off?" he inquired. For him, it wasn't even about "You've got to show those guys." It was more straightforward: "You're a musician and a singer, so that's what you do."

He has a collection of rhythms and global music that he has accumulated over the years and carries with him. He had Egyptian, African, and South American music, among other types. He continued playing music that I'd never heard before. It was extremely motivating. I pulled up a guitar and began jamming, and we had written around four or five ideas in no time. He came over every day, rolling up a big one. They've also got excellent things over there. I didn't smoke as much as he did, but he'd get high and get me heated up.

I turned around and returned to California. I went up to Mickey's house, and the two of us cranked up the African music to maximum volume. I played guitar, he played drums, and we jammed for approximately three days. "Marching to Mars" was the only tune that resonated with me, but I became intrigued in doing various types of grooves. I found myself attracted back to creating a record. Mickey agreed to co-produce it with me. I started thinking about forming a band. I'd just gotten out of the frying pan when Mickey dragged me back into it. I would have stayed in Hawaii for months if he hadn't been on that plane. When we entered the studio, Mickey went completely insane. He never slowed down. He kept adding overdubs until he needed to bring in another recorder. For one of our songs, "Marching to Mars," he brought in four twenty-four track machines and used all ninety-six tracks. At four a.m., Hart was on the phone attempting to locate another twenty-four-track session when engineer Mike Clink from the Guns N' Roses sessions eventually remarked, "That's enough."

This one song took longer to complete and was costing more than the entire album. I made the mistake of instructing Mickey to come to a halt.

"You've wasted enough time and money on this one track," I pointed out. He was so offended that he went outside, sat in his car, pulled down the windows, and smoked a joint. Nobody was able to locate him. When I got out to the car, there he was, pouting. I expressed my regret.

"It's four o'clock in the morning," I explained. "We're all worn out." We completed the track, the last cut on the album, which had been completed for over three months except for this one final track. I really like him. He might be the most energetic, hardworking, and enthusiastic person I've ever encountered.

Marching to Mars included Denny Carmassi of Montrose on drums, Bootsy Collins of Huey Lewis and the News on bass on a couple of tunes, and John Pierce of Huey Lewis and the News on the rest. Jesse Harms played keyboards, and engineer Mike Clink also contributed. I got into the studio and crafted the greatest record I could, an artsy record that was a severe left turn for Van Halen. It was one of my best solo records to date. Every song is fantastic.

I paid for the album myself and didn't want record labels involved until I was finished. I secured a deal with a new label controlled by Sid Sheinberg, the former head of MCA, for the release of Marching to Mars. He'd retired and founded the Bubble Factory, a film production company, and the Track Factory, a record label. They provided me with a substantial advance as well as a lot of points. I was the label's sole act, and they would do whatever I wanted. It felt like a fantasy had come true. We held a press event in Hong Kong. We travelled to Japan and performed acoustic at a few in-stores. The record sold 44,000 copies in its first week—not chicken feed, but hardly millions. The company went bankrupt the following week. They'd released a big-budget film starring Bette Midler, which tanked, and that was the end of it. They closed their doors. The impetus was lost when MCA took over. The recording was completed. In the end, it did well, but it was a letdown for me because I came from a band that sold 5 to 7 million copies. Marching to Mars sold approximately 400,000 copies. I had a long fall. However, it was a successful record in its own right. The Track Factory wasn't the only choice. There was another man who wanted to sign me to the Disney label Hollywood Records. He slept on my floor for four days while attempting to get me to sign a record deal. On a cocktail napkin, he drew up a deal. It was a lot of money, far more than the other guys, but I had to pull out at the last minute. He was insane. On the cover, he planned to have a van with the word HAGAR written on the side. He planned to take the van around the country and give it away in a contest at the end.

I made the decision to form a band. I wanted someone who was the polar antithesis of Eddie Van Halen. Every guy I auditioned for did Eddie's five-finger tapping. When someone did that, they were done immediately. I wanted a black guitarist who sounded more like Jimi

Hendrix or Stevie Ray Vaughan. Vic Johnson of the Bus Boys was said to be a big Montrose freak. I flew him here from Los Angeles for the audition. I asked him whether he was familiar with "Three Lock Box." "Hell, yeah," he responded as he walked away. I hired him right away. I brought back David Lauser on drums and Jesse Harms on keyboards. During this time, Jesse was really crucial to my music. He encouraged my music by creating bridges and choruses, and he was a soulful voice, however we had a falling out and I dismissed him. I needed a female bass player, which is difficult to locate. White Zombie possessed one. David Lauser tracked down Mona Gnader. She was living in the middle of nowhere near Willits, California. She arrived at my place on a Harley, her bass fastened to the sissy bar. She may also play her a$$ off. One thing I liked about Mona was that she reminded me of Michael Anthony's twin. She is left-handed, yet she plays right. She's roughly the same size as a fireplug. They share the same high voice. They're like siblings from another mother.

I became a better singer as soon as Mona joined my band. Most bass players, like Michael Anthony, bang their instruments until they are out of tune. Singers, whether they realise it or not, acquire their notes from the bass. You may believe you're listening to the piano or guitar, but the moment the bass begins to play, you're singing to it. Mona has little fingers and plays softly like Paul McCartney. She turns up the volume on the amplifier, but only lightly taps the strings. Suddenly, I find myself singing perfectly in tune. Kari needed to spruce up Mona a little. Mona only wore a pair of shorts, a pair of pants, motorcycle boots, and a T-shirt, and she never wore lipstick or makeup.

Before the tour, I decided I wanted to dress like Janis Joplin, so I went to Haight Street and bought crushed-velvet stretch pants. In this band with a biker lady and a black guy, I was going to go hippie. I didn't want a heavy metal or glitzy rock band. It took a while for me to figure out who we were, but I knew I had this amazing, weird little band called the Waboritas—later shortened to the Wabos—and we rehearsed every day.

We performed 142 gigs that year. I went to St. Louis promoters Louis Messina and Irv Zuckerman, the two guys most responsible for breaking me way back when, and arranged for them to co-produce the entire tour. I played three-thousand-seat theatres in every city across the country, performing 142 shows that year and another 138 the next year. We went from door to door. "I am back," I said everywhere we went. "I'm back." It was the most difficult work I'd ever done, twice as hard as Van Halen. I kept meaning to slow down, but instead I kept accelerating. I'm not sure what's wrong with me.

For the first two weeks of the tour, I tried taking a bus. We played virtually every night. I couldn't sleep when I got back on the bus. I hired an eight-seat turboprop Beech 200 plane. It was pricey in comparison to how much we were earning in the theatre. I was transporting a large production. I hired Jonathan Smeeton, who created all those famous Peter Gabriel concerts, because he knew how to make a single truck's worth of gear look massive. He was also an excellent lighting designer, but all of this came at a high cost. I wasn't concerned with how much money I was making on tour. I was only attempting to re-enter the game.

Kari adored our band, and everyone adored Kama. On the plane, Vic Johnson would sit on Mama's lap. That's how we did things. We all piled into this jet, every seat taken, tour manager on the toilet in the back, and flew across the country. While on the road, we were trying to write songs for a second album. I wanted to do things the traditional way. We went to Cabo when we weren't touring. That's where we began to figure out who we were and create the party.

I decided to create my own tequila for the cantina. When I was looking for furniture for the cantina in Guadalajara, I had my first taste of true tequila. At the time, 100 percent agave brands were not accessible in the United States, as they are now. I'd always enjoyed the tequila ritual—the salt, the hit, the lime. When you're out with your buddies, that's a lot of fun. But with decent tequila, you don't have to. Like having a salad before a steak, the salt is crucial for the first taste to clear your palette. things simply set things up. I was ecstatic when I first tried authentic tequila.

It was challenging just to find agave growers who would create it for me. Most of them sold their crops to large manufacturers, and if they saved any for themselves, they prepared tiny quantities, such as twenty cases, for friends and family to drink. I eventually found a farmer who agreed to do it in brand-new five-gallon gas cans and plastic bottles. We transferred the tequila to oak barrels, which we purchased specifically for ageing tequila, and poured it straight from the barrel.

Despite the fact that I had only recently begun producing tequila, Kari and I continued to visit Maui whenever we could. I reconnected with Alice Cooper's manager, Shep Gordon, who lived on Maui and operated one of the island's best restaurants. He liked the tequila I showed him. Willie Nelson, who also has a property on the island, came over to Shep's to sample the tequila. "That's some damn good tequila," he exclaimed.

I had some porcelain bottles produced, and we began bottling the product. Shep Gordon found a distributor in Hawaii, and we sent out a hundred cases as a trial run. The corks would not fit, and the bottles would crack. Half of the cases were delivered backwards. It was a shambles. We started creating hand-blown glass bottles and delivering more cases until we got it correct. However, our manufacturer got into difficulty with the Mexican government, who took some of their property for delinquent taxes and demanded a million dollars to proceed. We began looking for a new grower.

That's when we came across the Riveras, a family of three generations, the grandpa, father, and son, all working together in the fields. They had no factories at all. In the field, mules were pushing carts. These people would dig a hole in the ground, light a fire, and cook the agave right there on the spot. Their tequilas were hallucinogenic and smokier, but uneven. Every batch was unique. They'd hit on something every now and then.

Shep Gordon struck an agreement with Wilson Daniels, a high-end wine dealer, in 1999. I knew who they were because Capitol Records president Bhaskar Menon had given me a case of 1966 Pichon Lalande Bordeaux for Christmas. These guys worked with wines like Échezeaux, La Tâche, Romanée-Conti, and Richebourg, which are so good and scarce in production that consumers are thrilled just to get a couple of bottles, much alone a couple of cases. They wanted to get into the spirits business and ordered 6,000 cases of Cabo Wabo. The Riveras had to stand up to the plate to deliver. They were used to producing twenty to fifty cases per year, but they made it.

Around this time, I ran across Narada Michael Walden, the Marin County record producer responsible for Whitney Houston's enormous hits like "How Will I Know" and so on. He stated he wanted to produce me, and I asked him what he would do if I allowed him. He ordered me to go choose my favourite rock song, loop it, and compose a new song to it. Rappers were all doing it— Tone Loc's "Funky Cold Medina" featured "Rock Candy." Gary Glitter's "Rock and Roll Part Two" was the first song that came to mind. "Great fucking idea," I think.

Jesse Harms looped it, then I wrote "Mas Tequila." Lauser played the drums in my small basement studio. Everyone at MCA became ecstatic. We recorded our second album, Red Voodoo, below, squeezed in, loving the small-time, basement studio vibe. I didn't mind whether the drums sounded bad or if there was leaking. That was the magic I was looking for if it was a good take. It was the polar opposite of the March to Mars. Shep arrived at Cabo. We visited the factory. He arrived at the cantina. He noticed the band. I had this 100 percent agave tequila that shocked everyone who tried it. He noticed me in a bathing suit and Mona in shorts and flip-flops onstage. "Roll it all together," he instructed.

It all made sense. Bring the lifestyle to life on stage. It was part of who we were. We were about to crack open the tequila. It all came together.

I'd heard of Jimmy Buffett but had no idea what he was about. Kari quickly recognized the connection and took me to a Jimmy Buffet concert at Mountain View's Shoreline Amphitheatre. I asked Jonathan Smeeton, who had done an excellent job on the previous tour, to build a set that looked like the Cabo Wabo. He went down for a week, took pictures, drew sketches, and returned with a stage. He's brought the audience onto the stage. He's got the palm trees, the palapa roof, the whole shebang.

"Mas Tequila" is a massive hit—most adds the first week, fastest rock radio track to the top of the charts, stayed there for weeks, one of the year's big singles in 1999. (After the song was released, I was only given one-third of the songwriting credit, despite the fact that I removed the loop and reversed the chord change. The take was shared by MCA's lawyers with Gary Glitter and his songwriting collaborator.)

Shep Gordon persuaded Hard Rock Cafe to host a promotional tour. He persuaded MCA to pay. We did fourteen cities, free concerts, radio station tie-ins, you name it, and we released the tequila. We sold 37,500 cases in the first year, making us the country's second best-selling premium brand. Tanqueray gin, for example, only sells 50,000 cases.

Looking back, I can see that I wanted to be a small-time band again, to move away from the massive Van Halen size. I wanted to go back to being a club band and include the Cabo Wabo spirit into everything. We had a great time playing down there. We'd go down there on our days off and have a great time. We'd play in the cantina for gratis. The place was always full. Everyone was inebriated. Nobody cared what we were doing. I'd had enough of that big-time Van Halen nonsense.

When we went on tour, I opened the performance by going out in front of a closed curtain wearing shorts, shades, a tank top, and flip-flops, with the house lights turned on. I'd introduce the Wabos, then have a waitress in a bikini bring me the ingredients for a cocktail. I'd finish with a shot of tequila. "This is how you do it," I'd say. "You put a little Cabo in there." When I replied "cheers," the band broke into an a cappella rendition of "Cabo Wabo." It was a novel experience for my audience. That was the Wabos' creation. We evolved into the people we are today. This is how I live. This is my diet. This is what I consume. This is how I behave. This is how I play. These are the types of music I perform. When we found ourselves, the whole birthday bash thing took off.

The Cabo Wabo evolved into a location where everyone could come and play. I never charged for my birthday celebration. It meant a lot to me. I brought my entire family, including my brothers and sisters and their families. Slash, Alice Cooper, Rob Zombie, Mickey Hart, Bob Weir, Stephen Stills, Guns N' Roses drummer Matt Sorum and bassist Duff McKagan, Jerry Cantrell from Alice in Chains, Billy Duffy from the Cult, and, of course, Michael Anthony began to turn up. Chad Smith, the drummer for the Red Hot Chili Peppers, began to arrive. Toby Keith comes to my birthday every year. Kenny Chesney came down with his entire band one year and played for three hours and forty minutes. He holds the record for the longest time spent playing at the Cabo Wabo. He wore me out with songs like "Eagles Fly," "Fall in Love Again," and several Van Halen favourites. He continues to insist that the only reason he left the stage was to pee. He'd had a lot of beer up there.

The Who's John Entwistle owned a timeshare down there. His birthday was on October 9, the same day as my brother's. He came down every year for my birthday celebration, which generally lasted two weeks or more. Entwistle was a party animal. We must have played there five years in a row. He visited my residence in the year before he died. He was completely deaf. Because his hearing aids were so loud, he talked quite quietly. When he took them out to change the batteries, they screeched louder than the surf breaking outside my deck. I couldn't believe he hadn't noticed. He replaced them as if nothing had happened. What a kind guy. Most of the time, he was high. John was usually holding a drink and a cigarette. He didn't stroll around with his hands in his pockets. He donned snakeskin boots, tight jeans with spiders on them, flamboyant shirts, and large vintage sunglasses.

"Oh, man, I can't sing," he'd say when I tried to get him to sing "Boris the Spider." We'd play Who songs like "My Generation," "Won't Be Fooled Again," and "Summertime Blues." When John was around, I was usually playing guitar. I had a lot of fun performing Who tunes with John. He had a lot of talent. I'd never seen someone with fingertips like his. He'd take Mona's or Mikey's amp and blow it up. Each and every time. I have some nice photos of John on the cantina wall.

Stephen Stills came down one year. There were already a few individuals there, including Matt Sorum, Michael Anthony, Jerry Cantrell, and a handful of Metallica members, drummer Lars Ulrich and guitarist Kirk Hammet, as well as my entire band.

Stephen's tour manager had called ahead of time. I told him how delighted we were to see Stephen and if there was anything I could get him.

"Stephen likes coke," he explained.

Stills arrived about midnight. Lars Ulrich, Jerry Cantrell, and I had previously performed a set. He enters the room wearing a tweed wool jacket. It's 110 degrees outside. He's wearing long pants and boots, sweating profusely, and dragging his overweight ass up the steps. I'm a huge admirer, but this guy is insane. I take him into the restroom and hand him a gram of cocaine that I had someone get for me. He opens it, closes it, throws it on the ground, and pulls out a Bayer aspirin bottle full of coke from his pocket. "I've got one of my own," he explained. Pow...pow, he tapped out a bottle cap for each nostril. I did some work. It was quite effective. Later, a guy who tried some said it was so strong that you touched it and your face went numb. Everyone buried their heels in.

We went outside, and Stephen began playing "Crossroads." Matt Sorum played the drums, Jerry Cantrell and I played the guitar, and Michael Anthony played the bass. Lars moved in behind the drum set after a while, and Stephen played "For What It's Worth." Lars didn't recognize the melody, so he began pounding on stuff. Stephen paused the music. "Where's that other drummer?" he wondered. "Get that other drummer down here." Lars almost crawled offstage. But Stephen remained calm. He was unconcerned. He was looking for the other drummer. Then those people went missing for three days. They vanished. They went out that night, went somewhere, and did not return. That's not how I hang around. I found out what had transpired when they returned. All the young bucks stated Stephen took them down and showed them. "He put all of us to shame," Lars said. "We saw the sun come up three times."

I attempted to meet with Stephen again the next night. I walked over to this penthouse where he was staying and brought two acoustic guitars. He's a fantastic acoustic guitarist, and I wanted to pick his brain about some of his tunings and possibly collaborate on a tune. We were so high by the time we took up the guitars that they were unusable. I tried to present him with a song idea, but he was uninterested. Then he'd try to show me something, to which I'd respond, "Okay, well, maybe, no, next." There was no relationship. I adore Stephen, but he's a difficult person to speak with.

"What's the deal with Steve?" I inquired about his tour manager. "He lights me up. He'll turn around and walk away if you say anything to him."

"He can't hear," he said. "He probably doesn't even know you said anything."

I boarded the plane to return home (I was flying commercial) and looked across the tarmac. Stephen is limping his way to the plane, dragging his leg like a mummy. He's still dressed in the tweed sport coat—he hasn't changed his attire in a long time. He took a seat across the aisle in the first-class cabin, one row ahead. He didn't even look at me. Finally, he recognized me and said hi, but he was silent and unresponsive. His leg was clearly in pain. Then it hit me—all the seafood, dehydration, whiskey, and blow—this animal has gout. I'm done with it. I understand how you feel. He'd been eating rock clams and shrimp and lobster. I bring everything into the dressing room. We had these fantastic seafood feasts. He was wearing that jacket and drank tequila like a fish. He probably didn't drink any water because he sweated so much. He claimed that on the plane, his leg was killing him. Gout, without a doubt. I abandoned him. When we arrived at customs, I completely abandoned him. I had no intention of going through customs with him. There was no telling what he had on him.

CHAPTER 11

ENTER IRVING

Johnny Barbis contacted me from a restaurant where he was having lunch. "Sam, have you ever met Irving?" he inquired. "Please have him call me."

Irving Azoff was the Eagles' infamous general manager. He was one of the most powerful people in the music industry. Barbis passed the phone to Irving, who lost no time saying the appropriate words. "You should make a lot more money than you are," he said.

He appeared to be a genuinely lovely guy. He urged me to call him if I ever needed help, and I soon asked him to look into a record deal I was about to sign. He returned with everything in order, including some pleasant small perks, and when I asked him what I owed him, he told me not to worry about it. He's a wise man. I went to his office for a meeting the next time I was in Los Angeles. Irving impressed me greatly. We were discussing my tequila business when he replied, "I know someone who might be able to help." Let's dial his number."

He picks up the phone, and with a click, he's on the line with someone. "Hey, Joe. I've got Sammy Hagar here." He's looking for tequila at Costco. "Do you think you can assist us?"

Irving is well-connected. He's astute and knows how to get things done. He took me under his wing and looked after me. I began to earn a little more money. Things are beginning to improve for me. If I have a problem, I call him, and the problem is solved. He possesses both strength and intelligence. The next thing I know, he's negotiating agreements for me, managing me, and collecting a cut. I never signed anything. Never even exchanged a handshake. He was, nevertheless, exceedingly fair. He did not bill for expenses. He would dispatch a member of his management staff named Tom Consolo. Consolo would fly in and out, acquire his own room and transportation, and pay his own way, and Irving would charge me 15% of the profit after production expenditures. Many managers take more than that. Irving was fantastic in my opinion. I felt comfortable doing anything at this point in my career. I didn't give a damn about my so-called image. I was open to all kinds of outlandish ideas. Irving and I were sitting in his office, planning a tour for the summer of 2002. We were talking about special guests and opening acts when someone asked if I had ever considered going out with Roth only to annoy Van Halen and get the fans riled up.

"What a great idea," I responded, "but he's never going to go for it."

"Let's see," Irving said as he picked up the phone. He called someone, and what do you know, Roth wants to meet with him. I'd never met Roth and had only spoken to him on the phone once, so I was taken aback when he stepped into Irving's office in full drag—big hat; shades; tight, shiny black costume with pants that flowed down over his boots. I didn't realise he was so tall until he sat down and crossed his legs, and I noticed he was wearing five-inch platform heels. I wore a T-shirt, shorts, and flip-flops. He sat stiffly on the chair, striving to keep himself taller than everyone else. I went to use the restroom.

"There has been a lot said between us," Roth admitted. "Let's forget about it and take it from here."

It would be his final act of cooperation. He rejected my offer that we sing a few songs together and make it a nice affair right away. He envisioned something more akin to a WWF SmackDown. We agreed to do the tour and agreed to alternate headlining—Roth one night, myself the next—with the first date picked by a coin flip, but every day after that brought another fresh demand from his staff. I was aware of his venture. A few years ago, a friend hired him for a

$10,000 show in Tahoe and kept contacting me during the show to tell me how far off-key he was and how horribly he was singing. Even though we both knew what he'd been painting during his solo presentations, Roth insisted on being paid the same as I was. He couldn't compete with my box office. He demanded ten times his current salary. Irving persuaded me to join him.

"You're just going to blow him off," Irving predicted. "He's got this scumbag cover band." The entire world will recognize that you are the superior of the two. Let's get out there and show it, Sammy. Don't be greedy right now. It is all about your future. All of the promoters will say, 'Sammy is better than him, and he's the one running the business, so we'll pay him more.' Going out with Dave will quadruple your money the next time you go out."

We arranged a news conference and flipped the coin, but Roth refused to back down. He was adamant on closing the shows in Los Angeles and New York. Irving worked it out by booking the performance for two nights in a smaller venue in Los Angeles, so we could each headline one night, but the booking at Jones Beach in New York fell through. Roth refused to give up, and I refused to let him win. On the excursion, we skipped New York. That was the case the entire time. Roth wasn't getting along too well. He had lost his voice and could no longer sing adequately. His weak band played only old Van Halen songs, while the Wabos and I were blazing through new songs and solo material, saving four or five Van Halen tunes for Michael Anthony. That delighted the audience. Roth never once invited Mike to play. My T-shirts were outselling him by a factor of four.

Ted Nugent and Kid Rock introduced me onstage in Detroit. Kid Rock brought me into Roth's dressing area after the show and questioned why we weren't singing any songs together. He claimed that by not doing it, we were ripping off the fans. We shook hands after Roth agreed to do it. When I sent the tour manager to visit him the next night about what songs we were going to sing, he returned and said Roth was upset and wouldn't get off the bus. When I approached Roth later, he said that he had stayed up all night with Kid Rock and couldn't sing.

"My throat," he explained. "Tomorrow."

He went through the motions again and again. It became a regular gag. "Hey, Dave, what are we going to do tonight?" I'd pound on his dressing room door. He would go to any length to gain attention. The Los Angeles Times dispatched a reporter to St. Louis, my top market, to do a feature about the tour. Roth refused to give the person an interview until I was about to go onstage. Instead, the reporter chose to watch my show. He acted like that throughout the tour. As we approached Fresno, Roth called to tell his bus had broken down. I had to either start the performance right now or wait until after midnight, beyond curfew, to headline. We went out and started the act, and he arrived just in time to follow us on stage. What a scumbag. He was tough to work with instead of being grateful for the enormous business we were doing, pulling him out of nowhere and placing him back on arena stages. I eventually let go of a reporter for the New York Post's Page Six story.

"He's a fucking bald-headed asshole," I added, referring to the swaggering, middle-aged prima donna who was out there attempting to be someone he wasn't. He's a nostalgic act that has to wear a wig that he spray-paints himself."

Roth noticed the piece while we were at the Verizon Wireless Amphitheatre in Charlotte, North Carolina. On his way to the showers, David Lauser walked by the dressing area, wrapped in a towel. "Hello, ladies," he introduced himself.

"Fuck you," yelled Roth. "Do you think I'm a faggot?" "You're a fucking fag."

When I heard the yelling, I came out of my dressing room. "Dave, you need to lighten up," I told him.

"Fuck you," he exclaimed.

A pair of roadies jumped between us, but Roth was accompanied by five huge bodyguards, who waded in and knocked the roadies to the ground. We phoned the police. Following that, a plywood barrier was installed to separate the dressing room at each gig. He couldn't come in until I was finished, and I couldn't come in until he was finished. I had anticipated that Roth and I going out together would jolt those Amsterdam dimwits into joining up for a stadium tour by Sam and Dave and Van Halen. It would have been the world's largest tour. That, however, was never going to happen. The Sam and Dave tour was a financial success, but it was a personal disaster. Despite the disappointment of the Roth tour, I continued to pursue other chances. When I was invited to play with the Dead on Valentine's Day 2003 at the Warfield Theater in San Francisco, the first time those guys got back together and utilised that name after Jerry died, I leaped at the chance. Kari and I had gone out to dinner the night before, so we were a touch overdressed, but just seeing the marquee reading THE DEAD was heavily on my mind. I went over to Bob Weir's house a few days before the event and he told me to choose a song to jam on during the show. I went with "Loose Lucy."

We discussed it backstage during the break. Phil Lesh was a great guy. When I inquired about the arrangement, Phil advised me to simply "feel it." I inquired as to how many bars remained before I began singing. "Come in whenever you want," he instructed. "When you come in, that'll be the verse."

I'd sat in with these guys before as the Other Ones, but I only played guitar on the final song, "Fire on the Mountain." The difference this time was that they were on my side. We made a fantastic rendition, and Deadhead tape dealers adore it. I sang a verse and then stopped. I looked around to see if somebody would cue me. These people were in their own world. They didn't give a damn. When I returned, everyone fell in line behind me. I genuinely felt what they were doing. I didn't think it was one of those goosebumps-inducing moments, but the audience welcomed me nevertheless. It wasn't like they gave me a standing ovation when they introduced me; it was more like, "Huh, what's he doing here?" But as I started singing, I could tell they were into it. Mountain Girl approached me as I exited and gave me a big embrace. I'd never met Garcia's grandmother, but I recognized her.

"Sammy, you totally owned that song," she added.

In the summer of 2003, I planned to go out with Lynyrd Skynyrd on their "Party of a Lifetime" tour, only to have surviving Skynyrd guitarist Gary Rossington fall from heart difficulties at the outset of the trip. The band cancelled a number of shows. I had the brilliant notion of reuniting Montrose as my special guests and continuing with the gigs on my own. I offered the three of them $10,000 per night to divide, with all costs paid, including a private jet and a road manager. Denny Carmassi and Bill Church leaped at the possibility. Ronnie Montrose was less enthusiastic.

"Okay, Hagar," he said, "but are you sure you got the private plane?"

It turned out really well. I finished my set and returned for the encore with Montrose. We performed "Rock the Nation," "Bad Motor Scooter," "Rock Candy," and "Space Station Number 5," and we were always rewarded with an encore. They were paid more than they'd ever been paid before, and there were times when we were very fucking good. But Ronnie began ego-tripping with my band, attempting to instruct my guitarist, Vic, where he could put his gear onstage and other silly nonsense. I suppose that was unavoidable, but I only did it a few more times.But Irving didn't stop there. He desired a Van Halen reunion, and since I was the sane one in the group and the guy he managed, he began working behind the scenes to make it happen. He persuaded Al to phone me on New Year's Eve 2003, the start of what turned out to be a very important year. I've always adored Al. Even after I left the band, he and I would occasionally call on our birthdays or New Year's Eve. It was a means for us to stay in touch even when things were awful. Since my departure, the brothers had done very little. They'd recorded an album with Gary Cherone, who later revealed to me that they'd auditioned him when I was still in the band. Ray Danniels was in charge of Cherone because he was in charge of Extreme. First, he sought to get Cherone into the Broadway production of Phantom of the Opera. Danniels later informed him that he would be the singer for Van Halen. Gary is a gifted individual. Good singer, in good physical condition, a healthy guy, not a druggie, and a truly cool guy. What went wrong for the band? Hundreds of times. Van Halen III was the only Van Halen album that did not achieve platinum status. Eddie, according to Gary, insisted on doing exactly what he was told on the record. He directed his singing and even authored some of the lyrics. He'd never done anything like that before. Ray Danniels once told me, "Eddie wants his band back." Eddie allegedly dismissed Al twice during the filming of Van Halen III. Eddie was the drummer. I always urged him he should record a solo album. Because of Ed and Al's state, it took years to complete the record.

I'm not sure how they did the tour, even the short one. Al couldn't stay on the field for too long. Eddie was limping. The Van Halen III tour did not do well financially. They cancelled numerous dates. In Sacramento, they served 1600 individuals. Eddie went off the stage after they had played for forty minutes. I wasn't present, but Gary informed me later we became friends. I invited him to join me for a free concert I gave for firefighters in New York's Irving Plaza after the World Trade Center was destroyed. He also said Eddie left the stage in the middle of a show in Boston and did not return for a half hour.

After the tour, they sacked Cherone and tried to rekindle their relationship with Roth, which did not endure. They attempted five abortions with Roth. They'd decide to get together, go on tour, or work on new material, but nothing ever came of it. I was aware of what was going on. I maintained contact with Michael Anthony.

Meanwhile, I was having a good time with the tequila. I didn't need the money from a reunion tour because the Cabo Wabo Cantina had turned into an oil well gushing money. The brothers, on the other hand, were a different story. They told me they were virtually out of money. Al had recently divorced and had lost a lot of money. He was mostly in debt when he divorced, but Al was deeply in debt when I quit the band. They'd made some poor business choices. They were running low on funds and desperately needed the money.

When Al contacted me on New Year's Eve 2003, I told him that Kari, the kids, and I were going to Laguna Beach and that he should come visit. He was accompanied by his new wife and their child. They arrived around noon and lasted until after midnight. We drank, laughed, and joked. Al sipped coffee, but I drank two glasses of wine. Al's phone rang late at night, and it was Ed who answered. He handed me the phone. Ed began to drill me.

"Why did you quit the band?" he inquired.

It was late in the evening. I assumed he was inebriated and shone it on him.

CHAPTER 12

SAMURAI HAIR

I had been waiting for him for more than an hour at Eddie's 5150 Studios. I hadn't seen him in over a decade. He appeared to have not washed in a week. He hadn't changed his clothes for at least that long. He wasn't dressed up. He had a massive overcoat and army pants that were worn and frayed at the cuffs and held up with a piece of rope. I'd never seen him look so thin in my life. He was missing several teeth, and the ones he did have were black. His boots were so worn out that he wrapped gaffer's tape across them, yet his big toe still protruded. He approached me, stooped down like an old guy, a cigarette in his mouth. Because of cancer, he had a third of his tongue removed, and he spoke with a minor lisp.

"Are you all right, man?" he inquired.

"I'm fine," I explained.

"Well, you look a little beat up," he commented.

I looked across at Al, who was laughing. In a way. I had the notion that I should get the fuck out of there—this guy is insane as a crazy. But he made the give-me-a-hug gesture, an awkward embrace to be sure. He was not just the strangest person I'd ever seen, but he was also the most torn up. But I hugged him anyway. If we were going to get along, I figured we should make a new record.

"Let's go play some music," I said. "Show me some stuff." "What do you have?"

He looked through all these tapes and played me a lot of song ideas, just him and Al improvising as usual. Some of it was pretty interesting. I was thinking, "I like that, I like this, I don't necessarily like that." I stayed for a few days and attempted to compose with them. The day would begin at noon at the latest. Eddie would sometimes not arrive at the studio until nine o'clock at night. He lived right next door. Al was going to go check on him.

"He had a hard time last night," Al would explain. "He was up all night trying to write songs."

He may have lost a portion of his tongue to cancer, but he continued to smoke cigarettes. He claimed the cancer was caused by putting the guitar pick in his mouth while playing with his fingers. I told him that smoke had murdered our manager, Ed Leffler, but he didn't believe me. He spent the entire day walking about, sipping cheap Shiraz straight from the bottle. That explains his black teeth. "Ed, why don't you get yourself a glass for that?" I said.

He raised the bottle. "It's in a glass," he confirmed. He was living with a pathologist, who was constantly slicing his tongue to check for malignancy. He overcame cancer. He informed me he treated himself by liquefying and injecting fragments of his tongue into his body. He also told me that when he had his hip replaced, he stayed awake throughout the procedure and assisted the physicians in drilling the hole. What a nutcase. I'm not sure what he was doing, but he seemed to go for three or four days at a time. On tour, he would hang out with one of our opening performers and visit their dressing area before the event. He kept whatever he was doing hidden. I didn't see what he was doing, but he was doing something. In addition to drinking wine all day. He'd never stay in one area for more than twenty minutes.

"I'll be right back," he'd promise. "I've got to pee." Gary Cherone informed me he did it once during a show.

His marriage had ended. Valerie had vanished. He finally asked me to his sixteen-thousand-square-foot mansion, which he and Valerie had built before their divorce. It appeared that vampires dwelt there. The floor was littered with bottles and cans. The handle on the refrigerator door was broken. It looked like a slum shack. There were spider webs all over the place. He had large blankets draped over the windows. For soundproofing, the mattresses were removed from the beds and leaned against the wall. He was composing music and experimenting with different sounds. He indicated we'd be recording a lot over there. He'd excavated a ditch to connect the studio to his residence. We never utilised it once in the three tracks we did eventually record. He was sleeping on the floor, surrounded by a blanket and a pillow. There was nothing in the cabinets. I'd never seen a dirtier environment in my life. It reminded me of the house in the movie Grey Gardens.

Eddie Van Halen was one of the nicest people I'd ever met. He'd become the strangest fuck I'd ever seen, vulgar, harsh, and unkempt. I should have walked, but Eddie has a very lovely, crafty side to him, and you get the impression he has a nice heart. He's going to show up. He'll clean up, and we'll get this thing finished.

Some of the music was excellent, but it was all recorded. It was more difficult to get him to play music. He began playing the song that became "Up for Breakfast" on the Greatest Hits album. The keyboard portion had already been captured digitally. Al and Eddie were going to perform live for me to demonstrate. I was holding a microphone. I was prepared to jam with them as usual. He started and then stopped.

"I've got to play the keyboard part," he admitted.

Ed would begin the song, then say, "Wait, wait, wait." "I need to replace my amplifier." He'd never get more than a few bars in. "Oh, no, no, hold on a second. This is not right. "I need to change guitars." He couldn't even get through the song. Al brought out a tape and played me an already recorded version around two hours later. What

I heard was fantastic. The keyboard passage reminded me of "Why Can't This Be Love" and another favourite of mine, "Mine All Mine."

However, the sessions were a disaster. Al was completely delusory. I tried to talk to Al about his brother, but he wouldn't listen.

"You know him," Al would reply, pointing to Eddie's hand-painted signature guitar. "See all those stripes and wacky things all over the place?" That is how his thinking operates. Everything is dispersed this way and that way. I can't concentrate. I'm having trouble concentrating."

We planned to record an album in three months, but it rapidly became clear that we only had three songs that were good enough, and there would be no album. Glen Ballard, who produced Alanis Morrisette's Jagged Little Pill, was brought in as a true pro who really wanted to make things happen. My lyrics were written. Eddie had stacks of cassette tapes. We found some old tapes—sessions with Cherone? Roth? I'm not sure—I cut and diced them into new tunes and wrote lyrics for them. We finished everything in one week. Ed spent three months completing the guitar parts for three songs and two solos. Eddie Van Halen, whom I first met, could have done it in an hour.

Ed came in with a C-clamp one day while I was there. Glen Ballard invited me to come down and be a part of all the sessions, to try to keep the atmosphere positive and to assist choreograph this thing—to really support him. He didn't want to be alone in there with this lunatic. Eddie wanted to play the Telecaster, but he couldn't get it to stay in tune. It played differently every time he tried it. Eddie moved the guitar to his workshop, C-clamped it to his workbench, and ran cables out of the studio down the driveway after they had been working on it for three or four days. Of course, that didn't work.

When I arrived at the studio at five o'clock in the afternoon, Ed had not yet arrived. I'd hang out, but by the time Eddie arrived at the studio at nine o'clock, I'd left. He would exhaust everyone by staying up all night working. When I tried to tell him about it, he looked at me as if I were insane. "You already know I can't do anything unless I'm creative," he explained. Ed decided he wanted to learn to play the bass. He refused to allow Mike to play bass on these three tunes. The bass section on one song, "It's About Time," took him at least a week to complete. Mike could have finished it in under one hour. That was all I needed to sing when they eventually laid down the rhythm guitar recordings. His guitar solos were unnecessary. I didn't require any of the additional production. I went in and hammered off my vocals on all three tracks in two hours as soon as they got that. Michael Anthony arrived, and we completed all of the backgrounds in another two hours. We were finished in half a day. Eddie was still sound sleeping. We were finished by the time he arrived. I left. They worked on Eddie's guitars for the following three months.

He dismissed the monitor guy, the sound guy, the piano tech, and at least five guitar techs just during rehearsals. Something is wrong when a guy blames everyone else, including the keyboard guy, who is simply pressing a button that activates the keyboard part. It was the wildest, most insane stuff. I could see it was going to be a disaster. I informed Irving.

Irving is a true professional. Irving knows how to get things done, yet he is not a confrontational person. He tended to schmooze things, but Irving agreed to stage an intervention with Eddie shortly after we began rehearsals. He arrived at 5150 with a large, burly security guard. Eddie entered the room, carrying his wine bottle. Irving did all of the speaking. He warned Eddie that the tour would be difficult, that he needed to go away for a week or two, and that we may postpone certain performances if necessary. Eddie needs to clean up, we all agreed. He shattered the bottle. "Fuck you," he exclaimed. "I'm going to kill the first motherfucker who tries to take this bottle from me." I abandoned my family for this nonsense. "Do you think I'm going to do this for you?"

That's how ill the cat was at the time. The tour was going to be lengthy. The first event in Greensboro, North Carolina, was incredible. Eddie wasn't spectacular, but he was adequate. David Fisher created a set based on a concept Al and I had of using the Van Halen rings to create special seating sections in the middle of the stage. It blew me away the first time I stepped out on that stage—the band was so powerful, and the people were so enthusiastic. That got me a long way.

But I couldn't listen to Eddie from the start of the tour. He made some bad blunders and appeared to be unable to recall the tunes. He'd just wheedle-wheedle-wheels on the whammy bar. To find my notes, I'd listen to Mikey.

He appeared messed up whenever he stepped out without a shirt and his hair tied up samurai-style. That was his discrete signal. I'm not sure what it was. He'd come out with his hair down initially, then go back to change guitars or during Al's drum solo, and come out with his hair up and shirt off. I'd look at Mike and roll my eyes—here we are again. He'd come out at the start of the show with his shirt off and his hair up on other evenings. He appeared to be a street bum. His hair had become matted. We boarded a plane after a show once, and he spent almost the whole journey in the restroom. When he finally emerged, he had this hairbrush with fur bristles wrapped up in his hair and hanging down. He was drenched, as if he had tried to take a bath in the aeroplane sink. I forced Kari to look at me. I didn't want the guy staring at me. He slumped on the floor, fussing with the brush trapped in his hair, and never returned to his seat. Hospital-crazy.

When we weren't travelling with our children, Kari and I shared this large Gulfstream jet with Eddie and his girlfriend, Al and his wife, Mikey, and some management and security personnel. Mike and I stayed over after one of the shows, like we usually do, and showered. Ed did not take a shower. He stepped into the limo shortly after leaving the stage and drove straight to the airport. Eddie was sitting there drinking his wine from the bottle when Mike and I arrived, laughing and joking and eating a couple of barbecue sandwiches we had ordered. He went crazy on us.

"Don't ever fucking make me wait," he said. "You're nothing without me." You require my assistance. You'll see what I mean. You will have nothing at the end of this tour. If you ever want to tour again, you'll have to contact me."

He was looking in one direction, while I was looking in the other. "Ed, shut the fuck up, man," I yelled as I turned around. Come on, people. We just finished a gig."

"Fuck you," he yelled, slamming his bottle against the plane window. One of the security guards attempted to calm him down, but he continued to rant and pound the bottle. I turned away from him.

Irving's office guy was staring at me, shaking his head and zipping his lips. The hostess and the pilot began to panic. They were hesitant to board the plane with this lunatic on board. Finally, Al convinced him to ease up, and we took off. When we got to the next hotel, Eddie began inquiring about my room number. He was unaware of the alias I used while checking into motels. The tour manager called my hotel phone and said Eddie was looking for me.

"Bring that motherfucker over here," I instructed. "I quit. This is completed. I'll be returning home tomorrow. I'm never going to work with him again. He's attempting to break the window out of a $40 million jet. He has no regard for anything or anyone. He's a jerk. "I'm finished with this tour."

I contacted my lawyer. When he read the contract I had signed, he was not pleased. It was designed by Irving and his attorney. Outside of life-threatening medical crises, I was responsible for all lost income if I cancelled any concerts. He estimated that leaving before I finished the gigs would cost $5 million. I was suffocated. Eddie apologised, but I would never travel with him again.

It was like the Sam and Dave tour all over again, but this time it was Sam and Eddie. They did everything they could to keep us apart. Irving was wiser. We flew in several jets. We stayed in various hotels. We had our own limo service. They were accompanied by bodyguards. Mike and I each had one. I remained in my dressing room on the opposite side of the hall. I just spotted him when we walked out onto the stage. I'd walk over to his dressing room before the show every now and then to see how he was, and it was generally fantastic. He'd start playing, and I'd start singing and jamming like it was old times. Other times, he'd start telling me ridiculous stories like, "I pulled my own tooth—this thing was bugging me so I got a pair of pliers and pulled it out."

I didn't think he'd be able to make it. I kept expecting each week to be the last. He was on his way to the hospital. He collapsed several times. He once told us that he had been hit by a car. He was lying down and couldn't get up because he was so messed up.

"I got hit by a car," he explained. "You guys don't understand."

He'd go till he passed out. Then he'd crash at a hotel for a day or two. He planned to wear the same outfit for a week. He'd sprint offstage without changing and head right up to his room. He'd be wearing the same outfit the next morning. That night onstage, I wore the same outfit. Throughout the tour, he wore those boots with the tape wrapped around them. His solo turned out to be a flop. It used to be the main attraction of every show. He'd now play nothing but crap. He'd try to play "Eruption," one of his best works, and blow it. He'd take the whammy bar, press the sustainer, and start producing all of this noise. The audience wasn't convinced either. I saw him perform alone several times. He would utter outrageous things to the audience. "I'm just fucking around," he'd explain. "I adore you all. You cover my rent."

This has gotten so awful. Al once threw drumsticks at him. He couldn't even stand up another time, so he sat on the drum riser. Al had thrown down a stick. He took up the drumstick and began playing his guitar solo with it. It sounded like a small child slamming on stuff. I didn't approach him onstage. There will be no more Jimmy Page and Robert Plant. I'm over here if he's over there. I'll go over there when he comes over here. There are no bad feelings, simply no vibes.

Ed appeared to be going through the motions, as if he didn't care about his performance. He didn't give a damn about his appearance. He simply went out and took the money. He was humiliating. Al, Mike, and I did it from the bottom of our hearts. Every night, we played our hearts out. Ed walked out there and jerked away. We went through three different sound engineers. After gigs, he'd grab a board mix and listen to it. Because he was playing so badly, the sound guy would hide his guitar. He was already playing so loudly onstage that he didn't need his guitar pumped over the main house speakers, but he'd crucify the sound-man and fire him the next day. Al and I would debate about getting him back, but it never worked.

They frequently shared a high school attitude. Every other band was despised by them. It was always a race with them. Everyone else was a jerk. I don't like everything, but I like music, and when I hear an artist I adore, I want to embrace him, welcome him backstage. Eddie was known for being a gruff wise-guy. On that tour, I went Kenny Chesney backstage and introduced him to Eddie. Eddie turned around and shook his hand.

"I need to pee," he remarked. He walked into the john, where the man was standing.

"Let's get out of here," remarked Kenny.

That was their only encounter. It was the first time I had met Kenny. We walked back to my dressing room and sat on the floor with acoustic guitars, singing "I'll Fall in Love Again," "Eagles Fly," and all the other songs he liked. We were drinking tequila and singing until three a.m. He became one of my closest companions. But Ed? "I've got to pee." That usually meant he was going to tie his hair up.

Toby Keith came to see us in Oklahoma City, not far from his hometown, another time. I chose to perform his "I Love This Bar" during my acoustic part and worked out the details with Toby. Even though I knew he was out of town, I was going to say that because he was from around here, I was going to do one of his songs. Then he'd come out in the middle of the song and sing the remainder of it with me. Toby later informed me that Eddie cornered him and tried to keep him from leaving while he was waiting backstage. "Why would you want to go on with him?" Ed inquired, according to Toby. "Why didn't you come out with us?"

"You didn't invite me," Toby pointed out.

"I'm inviting you right now," Eddie announced. "Why are you wearing that cowboy hat?"

"I'm a country guy," Toby explained.

"No, it's because you're bald," Eddie explained.

The place exploded as Toby went out on stage halfway through the song. Eddie went insane for the remainder of the night. After the show, he demolished his dressing room. Wolfie, his son, was terrified and wailing in my dressing room. I went to see if I could make him feel better. We left Ed in Oklahoma City with his tour manager and a handful of security guards that night and went to the next city without him. He kicked out the limousine window on the way back to the hotel.

"That boy needs help," remarked Toby, who went down to the gig in his truck with his wife and adolescent daughter.

Irving would come out frequently, but he would never approachEd. No one dared to approach Eddie, fearing that his departure might derail the entire trip. If he quit or went down, I'm sure the contract was worded the same way for him as it was for me. I could have walked if he had missed three straight appearances. He never missed a beat. Ed's work ethic was unwavering. The Van Halens are descended from hardworking Dutch stock. He was there every night, in the worst shape imaginable, but he put on the show. He was showing signs of rage against me. We marketed these deluxe thousand-dollar packages that included not just unique seating on stage, but also access to backstage, sound check, and catering. I never perform sound checks. I'm a performer. I save my voice for the performance. However, some of my followers purchased these packages and turned up in Cabo Wabo T-shirts. Eddie, according to Mikey, would target them. "Where'd you get that shirt?" he'd inquired. "What a piece of shit."

The remaining two performances took place at a small amphitheatre in Tucson. Eddie absolutely unravelled on the second night. He was aware that the tour was coming to a close. He knew he was over. When I was talking to Irving before the event, he approached me and rolled my sleeve down over my tattoo. I didn't even look at him. I simply rolled it back up. He rolled it down again. I rolled it up again.

"Don't be fucking with my shirt, dude," I warned.

"That thing ain't gonna last," he said, displaying his Van Halen tattoo. "Did you notice that?" That's a step forward. That will be more durable."

As if I cared. On the tour, we had a team of about 120 people. I had many cases of tequila in my dressing room and was sitting there signing bottles for the staff. Eddie walked in and noticed what I was doing. "Can I please have a bottle?" he inquired.

I walked to my refrigerator and took one out. "I'll give you a bottle," I said. "These others are all signed up for the crew."

He takes a couple of large slugs and places them down. "Why can't I have one of these?" he wondered. I informed him that those bottles were for the workers and that I had the correct number. I informed him that if he took one, someone else wouldn't receive one. He goes away, straight to one of my dressing-room companions, a booking agent Eddie recognized but mistook for Warner Bros. Records chairman Mo Ostin's son. He then proceeded to spit on this person over stuff that made no sense to anyone except Ed. "And your dad, he was a great man, and you and your brother are nothing."

He was really insane. He had previously attacked Valerie's brother, who had gone to the concert to see his ex-brother-in-law. In the dressing area, people were screaming and yelling, and he was racing around, beating up people and slamming bottles against the wall. He completely lost it.

Irving called me aside. "When this show's over," he said, "I'm getting you in a limo and we're getting out of here." My jet was waiting for me to return home.

We'd never done a worse show in our life. Eddie was terrible. My nephew was standing alongside me on the stage, watching Eddie perform his solo.

"I've never seen anything like this," he remarked. "What's wrong with him?"

He shattered his favourite guitar. Shrapnel was sprayed into the throng. He sobbed into the microphone. "You don't understand," he explained. "You guys pay my rent. "I adore you all."

They say he did something insane on the plane home. He was accompanied by his girlfriend and her two grown daughters. Al and his family were present. Mike and his wife chose to stay in Tucson instead of flying with Ed. Something strange happened on that airliner. My man was utterly gone and unconcerned. After the show, I went straight to my plane to return to San Francisco. After instructing him to keep his hand off my shirt, I never spoke to him again.

CHAPTER 13

GOING HOME

We relocated the entire family to Mexico before the start of the 2005 school year. Our kids, Kama and Samantha, were six months apart from my Cabo Wabo partner, Marco Monroy's daughters. In Cabo, we were neighbours, and our children were friends. We intended to enrol the girls in school while they were still young enough to acquire the language and become immersed in the culture. Kama was in fourth grade, and Samantha, her four-year-old sister, was in preschool. I was ready for the beach after a year of Van Halen misery.

We'd wake up to the sound of waves pounding outside our window. The weather was perfect. We had the Cabo Wabo and could eat at the cantina or have meals delivered to our house. We had maids, security, and gardeners working all around our house. Everyone needs a job down there, and they work hard for it. Life can be really comfortable.

When you go on a ten-day vacation, you spend the first seven days relaxing. When you go on vacation to stay, you will experience times of dullness before breaking through to new levels of relaxation. You've gone all the way down. We'd changed by the time we returned from spending the most of the year in Mexico. It wasn't only our clothes, though Kari and I noted when we stopped at the shop on the way home that the clothes we were wearing back in Marin County seemed a little worn and unclean. We'd arrived at a point that would have an impact on us for the rest of our lives. When we returned to the city and became busy again, we knew where that place was and it was much easier to find our way back there.

I kept the Wabos on full pay during the reunion. My birthday blowout at Cabo Wabo and the yearly weekend at the new Cabo Wabo Cantina that debuted in Harrah's Lake Tahoe in May 2004 were the only performances we'd done all year. Ted Nugent, Toby Keith, and Bob Weir joined me for the first time on opening weekend at the former South Shore Room, the large showcase off the casino where Elvis Presley and Frank Sinatra performed.

The Lake Tahoe cantina was part of a long-term growth strategy I had been working on. Don Marrandino, who worked for the Fertitta brothers and Station Casinos, approached me about establishing a Cabo Wabo in Las Vegas several years before. The Fertittas were fantastic. I became acquainted with them fairly well. The Fertittas purchased the Ultimate Fighting Championship, a type of extreme boxing that incorporated martial arts and no-holds-barred wrestling with boxing. They scheduled their first major encounter in the Trump Arena in Atlantic City, and I accompanied them. They dispatched a G4 private plane to fetch me up in San Francisco, followed by the rest of the party in Vegas. Because Atlantic City was closed due to a blizzard, we arrived in Philadelphia instead. The Ritz-Carlton put us in large suites. We went to a luxury Italian restaurant for supper, and they ordered the complete menu as well as cases of expensive wine. We flew into Atlantic City the next morning and attended their first fights. Station Casinos was founded by their father. He was the first non-Strip independent casino operator. He started small, but by the end of his career, he was running eleven casinos and generating more money than he would on the Strip. I thought these guys were the brightest individuals in Vegas.

Marrandino came over to my place to show me the blueprints. He wanted to build a Cabo Wabo complex, complete with an arena seating 8,000 people, a bowling alley, and a cantina. We were supposed to break ground in October 2001, but they changed their minds after 9/11. The contract had expired. Don Marrandino went to work at the Hard Rock Cafe initially, and then for Steve Wynn, who was building the Wynn. Marrandino eventually took over Harrah's at Lake Tahoe and immediately began planning to open a Cabo Wabo there. He has music business contacts and has engaged them to perform. He knows how to make a location trendy and cool. Most of these old casino guys have no idea what to do. "Where have Sammy and Frank gone?" The good guys are no longer alive. We don't have anyone to play with here." Marrandino was well aware that there was a whole new breed of individuals out there.

Originally, I intended for there to be only one Cabo Wabo. I despised Planet Hollywood, and when investors from Planet Hollywood and the Rainforest Cafe approached me about opening dozens of cantinas, I turned them down without even considering how much money I could make. The original held a particular place in my heart. But Marrandino persuaded me that we didn't have to be cookie-cutter, so we opened the Tahoe location (we've since expanded to Las Vegas). My annual Cinco de Mayo run with the Wabos in Tahoe has become a high point on my calendar every year, and the Tahoe cantina comes with this wonderful casino showroom. Tahoe's got a new Sammy.

For the Wabos, I created a brand-new studio in Marin County. I told them they needed to get together and practise at least once a week, but they were in and out of the studio all the time. They remained close. I was overjoyed to be back with the Wabos after the Van Halen reunion tour. After recalling the pressures on big-time rock bands, the high ticket prices, the massive production, the massive crews, and all that nonsense, I was relieved to return to a band that can just go perform. I brought the band down to Cabo to play for free in the cantina for a week. I spent almost the entire year in Cabo. I wrote "Feet in the Sand," "Living on the Coastline," and other songs for my next album, Living It Up, about pretty much everything I was doing.

When Irving called to tell me about Van Halen's induction into the Rock and Roll Hall of Fame, I was still healing from the reunion tour. He first stated that only the original band would be invited. Irving drove me insane. Roth was in the band longer than I was. He spent seven years with Van Halen. I worked with them for eleven years. I outsold him in record sales. How could they do such a thing to me? We had no idea the brothers were messing around with Roth again. Mikey and I were both on our way out. Irving returned the call and stated that everything was fine. It was most likely never a problem. One of the things he does is create issues in order to solve them.

Van Halen, R.E.M., Patti Smith, Grandmaster Flash, and Ronnie Spector were all there. I told Irving that we should all stick together and attend the event as a group. He returned with their message. "If you're not going, they're not going," he explained. I assumed they were bluffing. I half-expected Roth to burst in and do something dumb until I was halfway through my speech. Mikey and I were eager to play. Ed and Al called it quits at the last minute. Van Halen was set to be inducted into Velvet Revolver. Irving also managed them, which may have had an impact on how they got the job. Velvet Revolver planned a medley of one Dave song and one Sammy song in place of Van Halen's performance.

Roth called Slash, the guitarist for Velvet Revolver, and informed him that if the band played "Jump," Roth would come and sing with them. When Slash mentioned that the band didn't have a keyboard player, Roth urged him to record the section. He and Slash got into an argument. Slash informed Roth that they were a rock-and-roll band who played their own instruments and would not pretend to have a keyboard player especially for Roth. Slash volunteered to play "You Really Got Me," or "Runnin' with the Devil," but it was "Jump" or nothing for Roth. When Velvet Revolver frontman Scott Weiland learned of Roth's phone call, he informed Slash that he would leave the band if Roth was allowed anywhere near the stage. There was no way Mikey and I were going to join them for a couple of numbers by the time I called Slash. When I called Paul Shaffer, the event's maestro, he accepted my offer for Mike and me to perform "Why Can't This Be Love" with the house band. There was no way I was going to go without playing. Kenny Chesney insisted on accompanying me. Emeril Lagasse arrived by plane. Mike and I were there with our wives, and everyone was incredibly sweet to us. The photographer, Annie Leibovitz, approached me and hugged me. Keith Richards' daughter was interested in meeting me.

"I'll take a picture with you if you'll take me and introduce me to your dad," I said. I was dragged over to his table by her.

"Hey, mate, Sammy, good job," he said. I can't describe how I felt. It was the first time in my life that I felt valued in this industry.

I finished my speech. "I'm sorry the brothers and everyone aren't here," I explained. "God bless 'em, but you couldn't have kept me away from this with a shotgun."

At the end of the night, they created a jam based on Patti Smith's song "Power to the People." She's not my kind of girl (and I'm not her type of guy), but I recorded her song "Free Money" early in my career. Stephen Stills was up there, a little drunk, stepping on people and rolling across them. Eddie Vedder was there, and he was in fine shape. The members of R.E.M. were present. I was standing next to Keith Richards at the end of the jam. He winked as he stared at me.

"Good job, Sammy," he said. "Nice work, mate. Congratulations." That's quite cool.

Even so, the Van Halens would not leave me alone. That fall, I decided to go out with the Wabos and book small theatres, underplaying all of my greatest cities, with no more than two shows in each city, as a special surprise for my die-hard fans. Irving and I talked about the strategy. He agreed that it would help create enthusiasm, which the music industry sorely needed. Irving believed it would benefit the company the next time it went through the markets. We reserved the entire tour. We started hearing about another Van Halen reunion with Roth about this time. We didn't think that could happen. Mikey didn't think so, but he was replaced by Eddie's sixteen-year-old son, Wolfie, and the reunion began unexpectedly. The label put together another greatest-hits collection, this time featuring only Roth-era material. Irving ended up managing the band for the tour, and he put Van Halen right on top of me.

They both played in the same cities during the same week. They had either just left town or I had just left. It felt like we were on tour together. We still did well, selling out all of our dates, but it was such a dumb choice. Eddie and Dave obviously forced him to do it. Fans had waited a century for a reunion with Roth, and all the radio stations were buzzing about it. When I asked Irving about it, he pretended it wasn't a huge problem. He said the same thing about the Sam and Dave tour: show them how much better you are. When I questioned if he would send the Eagles out on top of Don Henley, he responded that it would be great since it would get people talking about Henley.

Irving, as much as I admire and appreciate him, couldn't help himself. He was making far more money on that massive Van Halen reunion tour than I was in those cinemas. I needed a new boss. I returned to Carter, the man who had signed me to my first record deal. We'd never lost touch, and he'd had a lot of success in management since his days at Capitol, most notably with Grammy-winning singer-songwriter Paula Cole.

The tequila business had essentially run itself while all of these trips were going on, but it had expanded to the point that I could tell it needed some serious management. My accountant took over the company, and he turned down an offer from a big-shot investor named Gary Shansby, who had billions of dollars to invest and previously controlled companies like Johnson's Wax, La Victoria Salsa, and Famous Amos Cookies. Shansby intended to pay $38 million for the tequila company, but the arrangement was difficult. He was only going to pay me half of what I was owed. I would keep a 50% stake in the company, and after he spent three years building it up, we would divide everything once he sold it for $160 million. When I asked him what he would change about the company, he replied, "Put some feet on the street."

My accountant was looking to sell. No, I didn't. It was one of the most heinous deals I'd ever witnessed. If his scheme failed and I wanted to purchase the company back, he would demand that I pay heavy-duty interest on the money he provided me for the sale. Nothing works. Shansby despised me for not selling and went on to launch his own tequila company. I turned around to my accountant, who was now controlling the company, and urged him to accomplish what Shansby had promised. The accountant employed a marketer. He put six regional salespeople in the field. He recruited a manager to oversee the salespeople. He established an office. That year, he spent $4 million on overhead. Nothing significant occurred.

Meanwhile, as my accountant, he landed me a restaurant deal in San Francisco. He contacted the other two investors, and the three of them travelled to Mexico to meet everyone at my plant, planning to launch their own brand. I began to suspect there was an issue. He sat me down and informed me that he and his investors wanted to acquire the company from me for $22 million. I had rejected Gary Shansby's $38 million offer. What on earth was this person thinking? I let go of my accountant. He did own a portion of the corporation. When he sued me for my shares in his San Francisco restaurant, I made a deal for his half of Cabo Wabo and he left. I hired a veteran of the liquor industry named Steve Kauffman to head the company. He was someone I knew who worked for Seagram and had done some consulting work for me. The poor bastard was going through his fourth divorce. He needed to get a job. The business exploded once he took charge.

Skyy Vodka approached Kauffman about buying the company a little more than a year after he started working for me. He had lunch with an old Skyy acquaintance and showed him the numbers. After lunch, he called and offered me $70 million for the company. I almost passed out. We were silent underachievers in the booze business. We had four workers. I didn't spend any money on marketing because we were doing well and growing at a good, modest pace. The three-year net profit averaged about $7 million every year. That much money made me joyful. I didn't require any further funds. I enjoyed keeping things guerilla and under control.

I visited the Skyy offices in San Francisco, which is a pretty cool company staffed by a lot of young people. I felt at ease and wanted to be a part of this group. I told them I might sell them half of the company. For approximately ten days, I went back and forth, waking up in the middle of the night thinking, "Oh, no, I can't sell this company." I eventually told them that I couldn't sell. I informed them that once I paid the lawyers, taxes, and bought out my partners, all I'd have left is a piece of money that wouldn't truly affect my life. "What amount would change your life?" they inquired.

"At least $100 million," I calculated.

They called again the next day and stated everything was fine. I couldn't even figure it out. What do you do with a hundred million dollars? It cannot be deposited in a bank. It was making me more scared than the fact that I was broke. I changed my mind and informed them that I would be unable to sell the company. That's when Luca Garavoglia, the young, handsome chairman of Campari Group, and his sidekick with the food stains on his shirt, Stefano Saccardi, arrived in Cabo for my birthday bash.

Luca could be the most impressive person I've ever met. He is a clever, sophisticated, and polished human being, graceful and elevated with a grasp of a wide range of details. He is a member of Ferrari's board of directors. When Luca was fresh out of university, his father died unexpectedly, and he took over the traditional Italian aperitif producers. He catapulted the company into the modern era. He began purchasing brands such as Skyy Vodka and brought the company public on the Italian stock exchange. The Campari Group rose to become one of the world's leading liquor corporations.

Luca and Stefano told me that because they ran a public company, it would be impossible for them to acquire only a portion of the tequila, but they could find a method for me to retain 20% of the company. I was perfectly fine. With someone like Luca Garavoglia as the company's owner, my 20 percent was going to be worth more than the 100 percent. Luca was the game changer. I completed the transaction in May 2007.

I took my entire family on a six-week trip to Italy, including my brother and his family. We spent a week at the Campari winery in Sardinia, which is one of the nicest places on the earth. We travelled from Sardinia to southern Italy, up the Amalfi coast, via Tuscany and Chianti, and into northern Italy to Lake Maggiore. We travelled to Milan to see Luca after spending a week by the lake.

He took me to the new Campari facility, which cost $100 million. Only approximately five workers were running the entire operation with this efficient new equipment that wrapped and sealed 250 cases of Campari in about two minutes. He told me some incredible figures—$15,000 every second or something—but he wasn't bragging. He was simply demonstrating. They probably had 6,000 employees twenty years ago. They now have a dozen, the majority of which are in the workplace.

"You ride with me," he remarked as we drove away from the factory. "Let's keep talking."

We climbed into his Maserati Quattroporte, which isn't all that wonderful. He was accompanied by two men. We took a seat at the back. The other two men sat up front. They had a look around, turned it on, and punched it. They were hauling ass 140 miles per hour down the freeway in no time. Every bump was felt, and I couldn't roll down the window. We were scorching. The air conditioner was not operating properly.

"I don't like this car very much," Luca said. "I like Mercedes, but I'm on the Ferrari board of directors, and they wanted me to drive one of their cars." The only four-seater is the Maserati. The Ferrari isn't for me because it doesn't have four doors."

We returned to the office and passed through a metal detector. The two other males took their pistols from their shoulder holsters. Nobody batted an eyelid. Luca's automobile rode so poorly because it was carrying 1600 kg of bulletproofing. A few years later, I began hearing about the new Ferrari 599 Fiorano. Ferrari enthusiasts compared it to the best of the best—the 275 GTB, the earliest Testarossas. I hadn't purchased a new Ferrari in quite some time. I made the decision to purchase one. I went to the Ferrari dealer and placed my order. When we were done, he informed me that there would be a two-and-a-half-year wait and a $300,000 premium over the sticker price. I dialled Luca's number.

"It's so funny you called me," he commented. "On Monday, the board will convene. I'll see what I can come up with. "What exactly are you looking for?"

On Monday night, I received an email from Luca, along with a letter from Ferrari's CEO, for the dealership. I received my automobile in two and a half months and paid full price. Ferrari even painted my car in black with a red stripe. They flipped the colour scheme on the interior—red with black stitching. They inserted a plaque that read, "THIS FIORANO WAS MADE FOR SAMMY HAGAR," and handed it to me on my birthday. The insignia on every other Ferrari is always a black horse on a yellow backdrop. They turned mine red.

Life was nice for an orange grove kid. I was wealthy and famous. I was inducted into the Rock and Roll Hall of Fame. I am fortunate to have a fantastic wife, wonderful children, and a loving family. I have achieved success in every aspect of my life. Cabo had been a long journey.

CHAPTER 14

WHO WANTS TO BE A BILLIONAIRE?

I'm having a hard time letting go of the record business. That has nothing to do with my job. It's a crying shame. People are unaware of how parched it has grown. The only ones selling records these days are brand-new small pop acts that kids buy. There is no record business for me. That hurts my heart. I'd like to set some records. That is a significant portion of what I do. But, even before Napster, I was looking for methods to avoid the large labels. I sent one album to the Tower Records folks, who were beginning a small label. For years, large corporations had cheated me out of money. I had just finished working with MCA and the Bubble Factory on Marching to Mars and Red Voodoo, both of which sold approximately 500,000 copies. I wasn't used to selling numbers like that, but I just wanted to make records. I saw it all go into the tank. I noticed record labels changing and not putting any effort into a person like myself.

You only need one new song. I recorded several recordings and issued them as singles, such as "Sam I Am" and "I'll Take You There," an old Staples Singers tune. I might have put them on a record later, but they were really just small gifts for the radio and my fans. I began spending my own money. I'd write a song, record it in my studio, publish it, hire a promoter, have him ship it to all the radio stations, pay a little money here and there, and get it played so I could have a new song. That was enjoyable but not profitable; however, I make money in other ways. Now I can have fun with my music.

Cabo Wabo's wonderful gift has been this. The tequila company allows me to continue working in the music industry. I could make money on tour, but I wouldn't fly in a private aircraft or stay in fancy hotels as an opening act or in small venues. I'm not going to make any records.

My band is compensated like a big-time band. I don't make a lot of money from my musical career, which makes me appreciate it even more. It takes the commercial aspect out of it. Taking the business out of my music has been the most successful thing I've done, because everything I do now comes from my heart, baby. I am also free to perform songs by the Staples Singers. I enjoy not being constrained by my image or what others think of me. That was a fantastic song. I was overjoyed to capture it. It was similar to "Sam I Am." I had the impression that I could compose and record whatever I wanted. In any case, there is no industry out there. In the end, I want to make records. I'd like to write music. I'd like to go out and perform new material for folks. One of the main reasons I put together Chickenfoot with Chad Smith on drums, Joe Satriani on guitar, and Michael Anthony on bass was for that reason.

Chad Smith of the Red Hot Chili Peppers had started coming down to the birthday bash every year some years before. He purchased a home down there. We'd jam, jam, jam. I told him he should never go to Cabo without first phoning me. I'd contact him and tell him I was heading to Cabo the next day, and he'd hop on a plane and go down. Every night, he, Michael Anthony, and I would play. Our tiny group was known as Chickenfoot. We performed cover songs. We could play whatever we wanted. I'd let Mike take the lead. We used to make an awesome mix of "Come Together" and "Give It Away" by the Red Hot Chili Peppers. We performed James Brown medleys, including "Hot Pants," "Give It Up," "Turn It Loose," and "Superbad" into "Cold Sweat." We were rocking and having a great time. Chad kept repeating himself. "This is it," he declared. "Let's start a band." It took me almost five years to see the light.

I promised myself I would never perform with another genius guitarist again, but I recognized this band required a superstar guitarist to work. I can't sing and play the guitar. That is far too much effort. I can jam, but if I had to do it every night, I'd be exhausted most of the time. Joe Satriani was the first person who came to mind.

When I called Satriani about playing together a few years ago, he said, "I don't play other people's music." But I'd seen him a couple times afterwards and he appeared very cool, aloof and quiet, remote and not overly outgoing. He was considerably more interested this time.

It was Super Bowl weekend in Las Vegas in 2008, and I had a gig at Pearl, the large lounge at the Palms Hotel. Serious amusement. We were completely sold out. Joe returned from his tour. We travelled to Vegas after picking up his amplifier. Mike and Chad were waiting for us. We chatted about it in the locker room—just talked. We didn't practise. We determined we all knew "Goin' Down," "Mr. Fantasy" by Traffic, and "Rock and Roll" by Led Zeppelin. We didn't talk about plans or anything. We simply got out there and did it. I performed with the Wabos, and for the encore, I announced that we would have some special guests, while the crew set up Joe's gear and adjusted Chad's drum kit. Mike's amplifier was already turned on.

That audience went through the roof after the first thirty seconds of "Goin' Down." I could feel it. It was felt by everyone onstage. Our wives, the workers, and management were all aware. It was felt by everyone in the hall. It was electrifying. I had just finished a tremendous night with my band, playing every possible song, but this band accomplished something special for that audience. This was a genuine band.

I knew we'd found an unattainable mix of musicianship and chemistry the first time we played. The nice thing about Chickenfoot was not just that the chemistry was instant, but also that we were all adults with our own occupations and money. It was unnecessary. We listened to music that we liked. We weren't attempting to be this or that. We were who and what we were, and we allowed whatever happened to happen. That made it similar to jazz in its own manner. It wasn't jazz, but it was similar to jazz in that we were four guys playing the music we wanted to play in the way we wanted to play it. It worked for us. I expected a so-called super-group to garner more attention. Record labels could support it, and we could go out and play completely new material, giving me a vacation from "I Can't Drive 55." I like the songs, but I don't like beating them up. The first Chickenfoot album was a success. It was certified as gold. We turned a profit. I find it difficult to spend a few hundred thousand dollars on a record and barely make a hundred dollars back, but that's the way it is. The record industry has effectively died.

I go solo in reverse. People like Phil Collins and Peter Gabriel leave bands to pursue solo careers. I've always started out solo and later joined a band. They decide to go solo since they are sick of being in a band. I join bands because I require motivation. In Montrose, I learned so much—how to play guitar like Ronnie, how to command a band, how bands work—that I applied it all to my solo career after Montrose. Ten years later, I was selling out numerous arenas, had five consecutive Geffen platinum albums, and was ready to join Van Halen when they asked. I was weary of doing my own thing, contemplating taking a year off, and having no idea what to do anyhow. I needed to be around other musicians to help me flourish once more. After ten years with Van Halen, I was ready to go solo once more. Unfortunately, I stayed for the eleventh year. That band had already taught me everything I needed to know.

Chad Smith of the Red Hot Chili Peppers had started coming down to the birthday bash every year some years before. He purchased a home down there. We'd jam, jam, jam. I told him he should never go to Cabo without first phoning me. I'd contact him and tell him I was heading to Cabo the next day, and he'd hop on a plane and go down. Every night, he, Michael Anthony, and I would play. Our tiny group was known as Chickenfoot. We performed cover songs. We could play whatever we wanted. I'd let Mike take the lead. We used to make an awesome mix of "Come Together" and "Give It Away" by the Red Hot Chili Peppers. We performed James Brown medleys, including "Hot Pants," "Give It Up," "Turn It Loose," and "Superbad" into "Cold Sweat." We were rocking and having a great time. Chad kept repeating himself. "This is it," he declared. "Let's start a band." It took me almost five years to see the light.

I promised myself I would never perform with another genius guitarist again, but I recognized this band required a superstar guitarist to work. I can't sing and play the guitar. That is far too much effort. I can jam, but if I had to do it every night, I'd be exhausted most of the time. Joe Satriani was the first person who came to mind.

When I called Satriani about playing together a few years ago, he said, "I don't play other people's music." But I'd seen him a couple times afterwards and he appeared very cool, aloof and quiet, remote and not overly outgoing. He was considerably more interested this time.

It was Super Bowl weekend in Las Vegas in 2008, and I had a gig at Pearl, the large lounge at the Palms Hotel. Serious amusement. We were completely sold out. Joe returned from his tour. We travelled to Vegas after picking up his amplifier. Mike and Chad were waiting for us. We chatted about it in the locker room—just talked. We didn't practise. We determined we all knew "Goin' Down," "Mr. Fantasy" by Traffic, and "Rock and Roll" by Led Zeppelin. We didn't talk about plans or anything. We simply got out there and did it. I performed with the Wabos, and for the encore, I announced that we would have some special guests, while the crew set up Joe's gear and adjusted Chad's drum kit. Mike's amplifier was already turned on.

That audience went through the roof after the first thirty seconds of "Goin' Down." I could feel it. It was felt by everyone onstage. Our wives, the workers, and management were all aware. It was felt by everyone in the hall. It was electrifying. I had just finished a tremendous night with my band, playing every possible song, but this band accomplished something special for that audience. This was a genuine band.

I knew we'd found an unattainable mix of musicianship and chemistry the first time we played. The nice thing about Chickenfoot was not just that the chemistry was instant, but also that we were all adults with our own occupations and money. It was unnecessary. We listened to music that we liked. We weren't attempting to be this or that. We were who and what we were, and we allowed whatever happened to happen. That made it similar to jazz in its own manner. It wasn't jazz, but it was similar to jazz in that we were four guys playing the music we wanted to play in the way we wanted to play it. It worked for us.

I expected a so-called super-group to garner more attention. Record labels could support it, and we could go out and play completely new material, giving me a vacation from "I Can't Drive 55." I like the songs, but I don't like beating them up. The first Chickenfoot album was a success. It was certified as gold. We turned a profit. I find it difficult to spend a few hundred thousand dollars on a record and barely make a hundred dollars back, but that's the way it is. The record industry has effectively died.

I go solo in reverse. People like Phil Collins and Peter Gabriel leave bands to pursue solo careers. I've always started out solo and later joined a band. They decide to go solo since they are sick of being in a band. I join bands because I require motivation. In Montrose, I learned so much—how to play guitar like Ronnie, how to command a band, how bands work—that I applied it all to my solo career after Montrose. Ten years later, I was selling out numerous arenas, had five consecutive Geffen platinum albums, and was ready to join Van Halen when they asked. I was weary of doing my own thing, contemplating taking a year off, and having no idea what to do anyhow. I needed to be around other musicians to help me flourish once more. After ten years with Van Halen, I was ready to go solo once more. Unfortunately, I stayed for the eleventh year. That band had already taught me everything I needed to know.

The contents of this book may not be copied, reproduced or transmitted without the express written permission of the author or publisher. Under no circumstances will the publisher or author be responsible or liable for any damages, compensation or monetary loss arising from the information contained in this book, whether directly or indirectly. .

Disclaimer Notice:

Although the author and publisher have made every effort to ensure the accuracy and completeness of the content, they do not, however, make any representations or warranties as to the accuracy, completeness, or reliability of the content. , suitability or availability of the information, products, services or related graphics contained in the book for any purpose. Readers are solely responsible for their use of the information contained in this book

Every effort has been made to make this book possible. If any omission or error has occurred unintentionally, the author and publisher will be happy to acknowledge it in upcoming versions.

Printed in Dunstable, United Kingdom

74401752R00087